ADVANCED TURKEY HUNTING

Richard Combs

OUTDOORSMAN'S EDGE™
Guide to

ADVANCED TURKEY HUNTING

Richard Combs

OUTDOORSMAN'S EDGE
OC
BOOK · CLUB

In Memoriam, Alec Combs, 1911-1987.
We'll not soon see another like him.

ISBN 0-9707493-2-5

Published by: Woods N' Water Inc., P.O. Box 65 Bellvale, NY 10912

Printed in the United States of America

10 9 8 7 6 5 4 3 2 1

Front and back cover and page ii photos by John Trout Jr.
Photo on page 21 by South Dakota Tourism/Chad Coppess.
Photos on pages 122 and 149 by South Dakota Tourism/Mark Kayser.
All other photos by author unless otherwise indicated.

TABLE OF CONTENTS

Foreword		**vii**
Chapter 1	**Scouting With a Purpose**	**1**
Chapter 2	**Hunting the Rut**	**13**
Chapter 3	**Hunting Funnels**	**23**
Chapter 4	**The Perfect Setup**	**27**
Chapter 5	**Advanced Calling Strategies**	**35**
Chapter 6	**Blinds**	**45**
Chapter 7	**Hunting With Muzzleloaders**	**57**
Chapter 8	**Bowhunting Turkeys**	**75**
Chapter 9	**Optics for Turkey Hunters**	**87**
Chapter 10	**Recovering Turkeys**	**93**
Chapter 11	**Guiding**	**99**
Chapter 12	**The Optimum Turkey Gun**	**107**
Chapter 13	**Hunting the Slam**	**115**
Chapter 14	**Leasing and Managing Small Hunting Properties**	**127**
Chapter 15	**The Trophy**	**135**
Chapter 16	**Fall Turkey Hunting**	**145**
Chapter 17	**Zen Turkey Hunting**	**151**
Chapter 18	**The Second Best Part of Turkey Hunting**	**157**

Acknowledgments

Friends always help in the production of a book, and it would be impossible to list all those who in some way contributed to this one. I owe a special thanks to the following:

Jean Findley, for her insightful editorial advice

Steve Gillen, for his counsel and encouragement

Tom Cross, who is at least partly to blame for my obsession with this wonderful sport

John Gilmore, for sharing his wonkish knowledge of what happens when a shot charge is sent down a barrel, and all the things that can go wrong between pulling the trigger and hitting the target.

Jay Cassell, for being in the right place at the right time.

Peter and Kate Fiduccia, for believing in this project.

And, for sharing their knowledge, their experience, and in some cases their hunting spots:

Larry Norton of Bent Creek Lodge in Jachin, Alabama
Jimmy McDaniel of Big Cypress Hunting Adventures
Jay Novacek
Joe Artimer
Tim Hooey
Tim Hart
Paul Meeks
Hank Strong

And last but far from least, my wife Claire, whose patience, support, and encouragement have made it possible for me to pursue a life most outdoorsmen can only dream of.

Foreword

Near the end of my fourth season of turkey hunting, on a glorious spring morning, I sat glassing a huge meadow atop a hill in southeastern Ohio. Dogwoods and redbuds bordered the meadow, over which flowed shadows of billowy cumulus clouds, and the new grass rippled in a soft breeze. All my attention, though, was on two gobblers, a jake, and two hens in a corner of the field. The gobblers were putting on a show, pausing from their strutting now and then to chase the jake whenever he got close to the hens.

For most of that season I had watched gobblers strutting in that meadow, almost always in the company of hens. Sometimes they gobbled in response to my calls, but with one exception they never moved in my direction. The exception was a gobbler that began moving my way from several hundred yards out, only to be intercepted by a hen when he had cut the distance in half.

In the three previous years I had hunted turkeys, I had filled my tag only once. I had read every book and magazine article about turkey hunting I could get my hands on. I had watched dozens of videos, and practiced my calling religiously with the aid of several good audio tapes. I had talked turkey hunting strategies endlessly with my more experienced friends. This was my last chance to get out that season, and I had tried every trick I had read or heard about.

At a glance, the meadow I was glassing appeared to be flat. As the turkeys moved across the field, though, it became apparent that there was a slight rise in the terrain--just enough that if the birds continued in the same direction, they would be out of sight over that rise, about 100 yards away. I waited until I could no longer see them, and began crawling across the meadow on a path to intercept them, pausing at the edge of the field to shuck my fanny pack. My binoculars were dragging, so I shucked them, too. Then my canteen started gurgling, so I unbuckled that and left it behind as well. Ten yards later, my owl hooter was digging into my leg, so I pulled it out of my pocket and dropped it. My pruning shears were next to go. Eventually I was halfway across the field, still on my belly, with enough hunting gear strewn behind me to open a sporting-goods store. Every five or ten yards, I stopped to yelp quietly a few times on my diaphragm call.

Finally, I could hear the big birds clucking and purring continuously, not twenty yards away. I clucked and purred back. After what seemed like a long time, I could see the tops of two tails fanned out, moving toward me slowly like sails coming over the horizon. They stopped, turning this way and that, and gradually sank below my line of sight. I clucked and purred again, a little louder, and they moved my way again. They never gobbled, but I could hear them drumming. Part of a tail rose over the horizon again, then all of it, then a head.

My safe was off, my finger was on the trigger, and I worked to control my breathing. Still, I couldn't see quite enough of the gobbler's head to risk a shot through the grass. I waited. The gobbler dropped into a half-strut, raising his head a little. I clucked, the head came up a few inches higher, and I pulled the trigger.

"Click." In a lifetime of hunting upland game, I had encountered at most two or three dud shotshells. Now, at the worst possible time, I had found another. I yanked back on the stock of the pump to chamber another shell and scrambled to my feet, with predictable results. The birds scattered. One flew off in the opposite direction, several others ran for cover. One of the gobblers, though, opted to bank around and fly for the closest line of trees, which happened to be behind me. It was a memorable sight--that big gobbler, beard swinging, red-white-and-blue head against the sky, flying by not thirty yards away. I shouldered my gun, swung, pulled the trigger, and was on the bird within seconds after he thumped the ground.

That moment was a turning point for me as a turkey hunter. Some hunters might argue that I had "bushwhacked" the bird, the implication being that I had taken him in an unsporting or even unethical manner. Their feeling is that the only proper way to shoot a turkey is to sit against a tree, call him into range, and shoot him on the ground.

I respect their opinions, but I disagree. I had put a lot of time into locating those birds; it was no accident I was in that spot at the right moment. I had used stalking skills I had gained in a lifetime of pursuing other species, and relied on my best hunter's instincts to get the birds within range. I had acted quickly when the situation required it, and turned bad luck into good luck.

The turkey that is brought in gobbling and double-gobbling, strutting, drumming, and pirouetting, epitomizes the classic turkey hunting scenario we turkey hunters live for. Truth be told, these are usually the easy gobblers.

At some point the persistent turkey hunter will began to take birds he would never have taken - probably would not even have seen - a few years before. They might be old gobblers that sneak in slowly and silently, requiring extreme patience. They might be subordinate toms that dash in from an unexpected direction in hopes of stealing a hen from the boss. They might be gobblers that strut and drum but seldom gobble. They might even be heavily pressured toms that have learned to move away from any kind of calling, and can only be taken by the hunter patient and woods-wise enough to bushwhack them as they walk down a familiar ridgeline or logging road.

Success in turkey hunting often hinges on the ability to remain silent and motionless for extended periods, then make a quick judgment and react instantly. Turkeys are notoriously unforgiving; wait too long, move too soon, misjudge the situation or the turkey's intent, and the game is usually over. Only by operating on an intuitive level can the turkey hunter remain constantly aware of his surroundings while at the same time focusing on his quarry and making the right judgments about when to call, when not to call, when to move, when to sit tight, and even when to pull the trigger or release the arrow.

It is my hope--and my belief--that this book can help you reach that level of intuitive hunting.

--Richard Combs, Cincinnati, Ohio, November 2000

"Whenever, in the course of the daily hunt, the red hunter comes upon a scene that is strikingly beautiful or sublime--a black thundercloud with the rainbow's glowing arch above the mountain, a white waterfall in the heart of a green gorge, a vast prairie tinged with the blood red of sunset--he pauses for an instant in the attitude of worship."

--Ohiyesa, Santee Dakota physician

Chapter 1

SCOUTING WITH A PURPOSE

Just as hunters should enter the woods on opening day with a strategy in mind, they should undertake pre-season scouting with a strategy as well. Properly done, scouting should enable the turkey hunter to:

1) Confirm the presence of a huntable turkey population in an area.

2) Become familiar with the geography of the area to be hunted.

3) Learn how turkeys use the area, patterning gobblers if possible.

4) Develop specific hunting strategies.

Confirming the Presence of Turkeys

Often, the first objective is achieved before serious scouting is necessary. A hunter might be familiar enough with an area to know that turkeys are present in huntable numbers, or might be able to rely on reports of other hunters or landowners. District offices of state divisions of wildlife, or their local equivalents, along with game wardens, are usually good sources of information on turkey populations. Members of the National Wild Turkey Federation (if you're not a member, you should be), can contact local chapters of that organization for useful information. With computers, hunters can search out hunting forums on the Internet and solicit feedback from local hunters. Local sheriffs can sometimes be good sources of information, also.

What exactly is a "huntable population"? That depends in part on the size of the parcel of land to be hunted, and on hunting pressure. If hunting pressure is very heavy, there cannot (in my opinion) be enough turkeys to represent a huntable population. Not only are chances for success diminished by the presence of too many hunters in the woods, but the quality of time a field is compromised as well, as hunting strategies are dictated more by other hunters than by the turkeys themselves. And nothing is more frustrating to the turkey hunter who has done his homework and caused all of 101 factors to fall perfectly into place than to have the hunt spoiled by another hunter No matter how good an area looks, and no matter how high the local turkey population, do yourself a favor and find a less crowded place to hunt. Better, in terms of both your hunting enjoyment and your chances for success, to hunt a small population of birds that are not heavily hunted than large numbers of birds that must run a gauntlet of hunters every day.

The size of the property you will hunt is a factor here, too. If you are limited to hunting a small parcel of real estate, your chances of success are low if population densities are not very high. On the other hand, if you have thousands of acres at your disposal, and can walk (or drive) to cover a lot of ground, even an area with a comparatively low population of birds can be productive. I tagged my first turkey on a wooded property of less than 100 acres. For several years I hunted the place regularly, and took a tom there every spring. My strategies were limited by the size of the place, but it didn't matter. Habitat in the area was a perfect blend of woodlots, cropland, and pastures. The turkey population was high, and the birds were always there.

By contrast, I also began hunting a state forest covering many thousands of areas at about the same time. Turkeys were dispersed widely throughout the area, and the population density was fair at best. Still, experienced hunters did well. There was plenty of room to spread out, and a hunter could walk for miles along ridgetops, or drive dirt roads, prospecting for birds.

Often, a hunter is aware that turkeys inhabit an area, but needs to determine relative population levels. There is no quick way to do that. If you are fortunate, in one outing you will hear sufficient numbers of birds gobbling, and find sufficient sign, to tell you that the population is high. More often you'll find a track here and there, a few droppings, and a feather or two. In most cases, at least several trips to an area will be required to get a real feel for the number of birds present. It's not unusual to scout an area and see only a little sign on one outing, only to return a few days later and see a great deal of sign. The time of year and recent weather must be taken into account. In late summer, or during the early fall deer season, there should be a fair number of feathers around, since the birds molt in the summer and the feathers are still present. Whatever the time of year, scouting after a recent rain is helpful.

Time of year is important for other reasons, too. Turkey ranges tend to vary between winter ranges and spring/summer ranges, though there will be some overlap. Assuming reasonable numbers of birds in an area, meadows, pastures, natural forest openings, logging roads, or cropfields, especially if surrounded by nesting cover, should draw and hold turkeys beginning some time in March in most parts of the country. In fall and winter, the birds may move into more heavily wooded areas where the mast crop is better, or to farms offering corn, soybeans, and other crops. This means that an area loaded with turkeys in the fall and winter may be nearly devoid of them in the spring. This is one reason it's important to scout close to opening day. If limited to one scouting trip, I'd want it to be within two weeks of the season opener, preferably within a few days.

Turkey feathers can be found anytime, but especially in late summer, early fall, after molting.

Learning the Lay of the Land

Gaining familiarity with an area is probably the best reason to scout in the winter, since scouting when the foliage is down allows you to get to know the lay of the land much faster. And just as deer hunters like to scout in late winter or early spring so they needn't worry about spooking deer, the turkey hunter can cover ground freely in the winter, when the birds are flocked up and when he needn't worry about alerting them to human presence.

Scouting in winter is the quickest way to learn the lay of the land and cover ground without fear of spooking turkeys.

Topo maps, plat maps, county road maps, and aerial photos all provide valuable information. Not all hunters take advantage of aerial photos, but they are available free or for a nominal fee from most agricultural extension offices. Plat maps are available from any county courthouse. Terraserver.com on the web is a good source of aerial photos. Coverage is not yet universal, but it soon will be.

While very useful, none of these can substitute for actually walking the property. The aim is to become familiar with every feature of the geography, including hills, ridges, points, creeks, draws, pastures, clearings, oak glades, thickets, evergreen stands, and fences. It is difficult to overstate the value of this knowledge in a hunting situation. The goal is that when he hears a turkey gobble on the property, the hunter will know where the bird is gobbling from, what is between him and the gobbler, which clearings or meadows the turkey is likely to head toward when he comes off the roost, and which logging road, trail, ridgetop, or fenceline, he is likely to use in getting there.

Patterning Gobblers

If turkeys were predictable, coyotes, owls, hawks, bobcats, and other predators would kill them all long before human hunters had a chance at them. Every experienced turkey hunter has found the perfect setup for a gobbler, only to have the bird fly off the roost and wander off, gobbling lustily, in a totally unpredicted direction, ignoring the most seductive yelps, purrs, and clucks. That's turkey hunting. Nonetheless, gobblers do have favorite roosting areas, strutting zones, midday loafing areas, and dusting areas. They tend to frequent these areas at certain times of the day, and in moving between them they tend to use the same haul roads, trails, fence openings, and creek crossings. (See Chapter 5, "Funnel Hunting.")

Specific knowledge about where these areas are, and how and when turkeys use them, is invaluable. Some forms of sign can indicate turkey patterns. The occasional track, scratching, loose feather, or dropping, indicates little except that a turkey was in the area, recently or not so recently, depending on the sign. Clearly a lot of tracks, feathers, scratchings, or droppings, including fresh sign and older sign, suggests an area that turkeys are using heavily and with some regularity.

Experienced hunters have little difficulty distinguishing gobbler tracks from hen tracks. The middle toe of a hen is usually two inches or less in length, though a big hen may be slightly bigger than two inches. By contrast, the middle toe of a gobbler is usually two and a half inches in length or more, and even a very small mature gobbler will have a middle toe at least two inches long. A gobbler's stride is about a foot, but closer to two feet when running. Drag marks in bare dirt or sand indicate that a gobbler has been strutting in that area, and you've probably found a strutting zone. Drag marks are not easily confused with anything else. They tend to be about two feet long, if conditions permit, and are parallel but not very straight. Dusting spots are good finds, since turkeys tend to use the same dusting areas repeatedly.

Turkey tracks - If the middle toe is 2" or longer, it's a tom.

These are often small, hollowed-out spots in dusty or sandy areas. Close inspection will usually reveal some small feathers in the dust. Because dusting is something turkeys often do at midday or later in the afternoon, these can be good fallback spots when morning strategies have failed. A big concentration of droppings usually indicates a regular roosting area. These aren't often found, and when they are, it's usually by accident.

Bill Massey, a turkey hunter from Indiana, was the first person to point out one interesting turkey sign to me. Bill, on several occasions, observed turkeys eating the buds from the tops of mayapple plants. Depending on their location, not all patches of mayapples will be budding out in turkey season, but those that are will often get attention from turkeys. Since learning of that, I've gotten in the habit of checking any patches of mayapples I come across. It is easy to see if the buds have been eaten the plant stems look as if they have been pinched off at the top. As far as I've been able to determine, while skunks, possums, and possibly some other creatures eat the ripe fruit of mayapples, nothing else bites off the buds.

Both gobblers and hens dust frequently. Look for tracks and feathers in dust for positive ID.

Some hunters find it difficult to distinguish turkey scratchings from the sign left by deer pawing for acorns, or even by squirrels and other rodents digging under the leaves to hide food or find it. Though old scratchings left by one or two birds can be difficult to identify with certainty, fresh turkey scratchings are usually easy to identify. One characteristic of turkey scratchings is that turkeys usually scratch all the way down to bare ground. If they encounter small roots, they like to scratch at the roots, leaving them exposed or broken. Typically, small piles of leaves are left behind each scratching. Some hunters believe they can tell the direction of travel this way, but that is not always easily done, since a flock of turkeys tends to mill about when moving through the woods scratching. It is difficult to confuse the fresh scratchings of a flock of turkeys with any other sign; generally a large patch of woods will be filled with scratched over spots, each with a small pile of leaves behind it.

Unlike deer, squirrels, and other woodland creatures, turkeys tend to scratch down to bare soil, often exposing small roots. Leaves piled at one end of scratchings are another giveaway.

An ability to age sign can be useful. Learning that skill takes time, but hunters coming across sign they know to be very fresh should examine it closely on subsequent visits to the area, keeping in mind rain and other weather patterns intervening between visits. Evidence as subtle as dew can indicate whether a track was made this morning or last night, as can the presence or absence of tiny cobwebs or insect trails in the track. Over time, hunters who examine and re-examine sign can develop an ability to age tracks, droppings, and even feathers.

Sometimes it is possible to elicit fresh sign by creating conditions favorable to it. For instance, if you find bare spots of ground at the intersection of two logging roads, a field edge, or another likely spot, soak that area with water from a nearby stream, pond, spring, or even your canteen, then check the spot a few days later for tracks. In an area that already holds tracks, hunters can eliminate the sign, then check back later for new tracks indicating recent and regular activity in that spot.

Depending on the accessibility of an area, it is possible to rake up hard ground, or even put down small patches of fresh dirt or sand in likely areas to look later for tracks, drag marks indicating strutting, or indications that birds are dusting there. The last and perhaps most important step in patterning gobblers is to visit the hunting area close to the season opener. Hunters should seek a good listening spot, usually on a hilltop, ridgeline, or bluff, and be there well before first light. Leave the calls home, except for an owl call, crow call, or other locater, which could prove useful. Be prepared to sit in one spot and listen for some time. Locating birds on the roost is fine-it gives you a general indication of where birds will be in the morning and, for those in states where all-day hunting is permitted, where they're likely to be in the late afternoon.

Even more important, though, is determining which direction turkeys take when they leave the roost. Obviously, the hunter who knows where the turkeys are going can be there waiting for them. Given that knowledge, it does not matter if the gobblers are henned.

Sometimes it is possible to elicit fresh sign by creating conditions favorable to it. For instance, if you find bare spots of ground at the intersection of two logging roads, a field edge, or another likely spot, soak that area with water from a nearby stream, pond, spring, or even your canteen, then check the spot a few days later for tracks. In an area that already holds tracks, hunters can eliminate the sign, then check back later for new tracks indicating recent and regular activity in that spot. Depending on the accessibility of an area, it is possible to rake up hard ground, or even put down small patches of fresh dirt or sand in likely areas to look later for tracks, drag marks indicating strutting, or indications that birds are dusting there.

The last and perhaps most important step in patterning gobblers is to visit the hunting area close to the season opener. Hunters should seek a good listening spot, usually on a hilltop, ridgeline, or bluff, and be there well before first light. Leave the calls home, except for an owl call, crow call, or other locator, which could prove useful. Be prepared to sit in one spot and listen for some time. Locating birds on the roost is fine - it gives you a general indication of where birds will be in the morning and, for those in states where all-day hunting is permitted, where they're likely to be in the late afternoon.

Even more important, though, is determining which direction turkeys take when they leave the roost. Obviously, the hunter who knows where the turkeys are going can be there waiting for them. Given that knowledge, it does not matter if the gobblers are henned up. It does not matter if they are subordinate toms afraid to respond to a hen call. It does not matter if they are old loners who will not come near a decoy. And it does not matter what the hens are doing or not doing. This is where knowing the lay of the land counts heavily. The hunter who knows the area well can quickly make an educated guess about where a gobbler is headed.

If the birds aren't vocal, or if they clam up soon after fly down, the hunter can use shock calls to try to elicit gobbles. Probably the most effective tactic is to pick a spot near a large meadow, a big, open wooded area, a logging road, or other vantage point, and glass for turkeys. Spotting turkeys not only reveals likely travel routes and feeding or strutting areas, but also gives hunters an opportunity to observe behavior. Is a boss gobbler alone, or does he have subordinate toms with him? Are gobblers strutting or not? Is there any fighting going on? Are hens coming to the toms in response to gobbling and strutting, or do they appear to be ignoring them? Are the birds in flocks, or do they appear as singles or as two or three birds together? Other chapters in this book deal with specific hunting strategies for specific situations, but all this information is useful in helping hunters formulate strategies.

It's important not to spook birds as the season approaches. The idea is to learn where the turkeys are without alerting them to your presence. Hiking ridgelines, walking logging roads, and moving from one spot to another in search of birds might be the way to go in large, comparatively remote forests, but a low-impact approach to scouting will serve most hunters on private land better. Any movement between one spot and another should be accomplished as unobtrusively as possible, using routes planned to minimize the likelihood of encountering turkeys.

Low-impact scouting close to season opener will locate and pattern turkeys.

Developing a Strategy

Turkey hunters typically enter the woods before daybreak. Planning to set up on the first gobbler they hear on the roost. When that bird has clammed up or wandered off the property where hunters can't pursue, they begin covering ground, pausing now and then to call and listen for a response. They may call more or less aggressively, depending on nothing more than whether they prefer more or less aggressive calling in general. It is hard to knock an approach to turkey hunting that has filled countless thousands of turkey tags. I've killed more than a few birds using that approach myself. But let's face it, the only difference between wandering around aimlessly and walking down a ridgeline or logging road is that the ridgeline or logging road gives us a sense of direction and hence an illusion that we have a strategy. In fact, it's a nonstrategy.

By contrast, the hunter who has scouted thoroughly and patterned the birds hunts with a strategy. He calls more or less aggressively based on his knowledge of how the birds are behaving in that area at that time. His initial set-up is more likely to result in success because he knows where the birds are, knows how to use the terrain and the cover to get close to birds without crowding or spooking them, and can make an educated guess about which way they will go from the roost. If a gobbler fails to come in, he quickly formulates a back-up plan, relocating to call from another spot, or determining where the turkey is going and getting there first. When gobbling activity falls off, he knows of a good strut zone or two, a place where he can set out decoys and call intermittently, with the knowledge that there is a good chance a gobbler will show up at some point in the morning. If he is aware of a spot where turkeys tend to seek shade when the sun gets high, he will be there waiting for them. He might know of an afternoon dusting area, and if he knows where the birds roost and can hunt all day, he'll know where to set up late in the day. He may have constructed blinds in some of these areas, allowing him to move in and set up quickly with minimal disturbance, and at the same time creating a well-concealed hide he can remain in comfortably for long periods. In addition, he knows how to move from one of these areas to another with the least risk of spooking turkeys.

Of course there is no guarantee that his strategy will pay off on any given day. Compared to wandering down a logging road, though, or simply sitting down in the woods in a spot that looks good, a well-planned strategy offers better chances for success. In the course of three or four hunts, the odds are on the side of the hunter with a sound strategy. Moreover, having a strategy offers the added advantage of being lower impact, not as likely to alarm birds and make them less vocal or more call shy. Having a strategy is particularly advantageous when the turkeys are not gobbling, whether it is because they are with hens, because the weather is bad, because they are extremely wary, or for whatever reason. That is when the hunter who has patterned turkeys can really take advantage of the knowledge he has acquired. Patterning gobblers is a time-consuming process that few hunters bother with, but done correctly it is one of the most effective steps a hunter can take toward filling his tag.

Tips

• One good way to find strut zones or other hotspots is to create conditions favorable for tracks or other signs in likely areas. Splash water from a stream or pond onto bare, dry earth nearby, or pour water from a canteen.

• Use a rake or sticks to rake up bare ground in likely spots, then look for tracks or drag marks.

• If the middle toe on a track is two and one-half inches or longer, the track was left by a gobbler.

Wide open spaces often make turkeys easier to locate, but harder to set up on. The turkey above is a South Dakota Merriams.

"Behold, my brothers, the spring has come; the earth has received the embraces of the sun and we shall soon see the results of that love!"

--Tatanka Yotanka (Sitting Bull)

Chapter 2

HUNTING THE RUT

No doubt someone reading this book glanced back at the cover to make sure they weren't reading a book on deer hunting when they saw the title of this chapter. Granted, turkeys don't rut - not technically speaking, anyway. They obviously have a breeding season, though, and that season is analogous in many ways to the rut with which deer hunters are so familiar. Nor is this an idle comparison. Turkey behavior is determined in large part by the various stages of the breeding season, and just as deer hunters must take the various stages of the rut into account when planning their hunting strategies and tactics, the experienced turkey hunter must do the same.

The turkey "rut," or breeding season, begins in late winter when the larger gobbler flocks begin to break up into smaller groups or even individuals, and the gobblers begin displaying and fighting to establish dominance. Gobbling activity picks up, and slowly builds toward a peak right before the majority of hens become responsive and begin mating. Frequently, Eastern gobblers travel in groups of two or three birds, one of which is dominant and does virtually all the breeding. Spring groups may be bigger than this, especially in the case of Rios and Merriams. In some cases, a single dominant gobbler will suppress mating activity and even gobbling by other toms over a surprisingly large area. Hens are initially uninterested in the gobblers, but at some point a little later in the winter or early spring the hen flocks will begin to break up also, and hens will begin establishing their own dominance hierarchies.

After that, depending in part on the latitude, hens will become responsive to the gobblers, and will go to them when they gobble and squat for mating activity when they strut. When hens become receptive, gobbling activity fades. The purpose of gobbling is to attract hens, so it only figures that when a tom has hens roosting close by who come to him at dawn and stay with him for at least an hour or two in the morning, gobbling activity will diminish.

Eventually, a given hen will lay her first egg. She then normally skips a day, then lays her second. She may skip another day between the second and third egg, but will then lay one egg each day until she has laid ten to twelve eggs. After the first few eggs are laid, she will spend almost all her time on the nest, usually in a weedy area or thicket, until the eggs are hatched, though she will take occasional short breaks away from the nest to eat and get water. Year-old hens will mate and lay eggs in much the same pattern, though they tend to do so slightly later than the mature hens. If a hen's nest is destroyed, she will renest again, and possibly even a third time. It isn't known if she mates again to establish a new nest. Once the eggs hatch, she will not nest again that season, whether or not the poults survive.

Hens traveling in groups, apart from gobblers, may indicate they are not yet responsive to gobblers-usually a good time to be in the turkey woods. (Note the nice beard on this hen.)

When the hens begin slipping off to their nests, and increasing numbers of them are spending time away from the gobblers, gobbling activity begins to increase again, building up to a second peak before tapering off again as spring fades into summer and hormone levels decline. At this time, gobblers begin forming the summer flocks that will grow and remain intact until the cycle begins again in late winter or early spring.

This cycle is of extreme importance to the hunter. Some state divisions of wildlife attempt to make their spring turkey seasons coincide with the second peak of gobbling activity. The reasoning is that hunting is good, since the now-lonely gobblers are responsive to hen calls, but the bulk of breeding activity is over, so taking gobblers will not significantly affect turkey reproduction. Not all states time their seasons this way, and in any case turkeys don't consult calendars, so the breeding cycle may easily vary by a week or more from one year to the next.

Hunting the "Pre-Rut"

I recently hunted Merriam's at the historic Clarke Ranch in western Nebraska. I was there to tape a segment for Cabela's Sportsman's Quest television program. We had only three days for the shoot, and show host Jay Novacek and I quickly discovered two things: One, the Clarke Ranch is absolutely loaded with turkeys, and two, our timing in hunting them was off-way off.

Traditionally, the Merriam's in that area are very huntable at the time of our hunt, but this year, perhaps because of unseasonably cold, cloudy weather, the birds weren't behaving. This is wide-open country, and spotting birds was not difficult. Through our binoculars we observed flocks of gobblers on the one hand, hen flocks on the other, with neither flocks showing a great deal of interest in the other. There was little gobbling activity except at first light and again at dusk. A few gobblers were occasionally strutting, more for the benefit of one another, it appeared, than for the hens, which ignored them. Despite what the calendar said, these birds seemed to think it was still winter.

We wasted a day and a half on traditional spring turkey hunting tactics, which only confirmed what our binoculars should already have told us: The gobblers were not in the least bit interested in our calling, or in our decoys. After that, it was a matter of learning the lay of the land and how the birds used it well enough to wait them out and bushwack them. That's a tough order when you've got a day and a half of hunting time to do it in. In the end we were defeated. We left with the feeling that we were just beginning to figure the turkeys out, convinced that in another day or two we could have bagged our birds, and confident that the hunters scheduled to arrive a week or so after our departure were destined to have successful hunts.

The point is that the turkey hunter must figure out as quickly as possible what stage of the breeding cycle the birds are in. Just as the deer hunter adopts different strategies for hunting the pre-rut, rut, and post-rut, the turkey hunter should employ different strategies depending on the stage of the birds' breeding cycle. It isn't always easy to figure out what's going on with the turkeys in one or two days. Gobbling activity, strutting, feeding, and movement in general are all affected by weather. Even at the peak of gobbling activity, rain or a sudden cold front can bring gobbling to a stop. It's also important to be aware that turkeys move around. It could be you didn't hear a gobble this morning because the turkeys simply didn't roost in the area you hunted.

Temporary changes in behavior brought on by bad weather, and the fact that turkeys move around, are among the reasons scouting immediately before the season opener is so important. Opening-day turkeys might very well not be doing whatever they were doing two weeks ago. Scouting a day or two right before the season opener gives you a jump on figuring them out. Had we had the opportunity to scout those Clarke Ranch Merriams a day or two before hunting them, we'd have started with different strategies. First, we'd have known the lay of the land a little better, and greatly increased our chances of being where the gobblers were going. That is always a good strategy, but when gobblers are unresponsive to hen calls it becomes even more important. Second, we'd not have wasted a lot of time setting up on gobblers and attempting to call them in with hen yelps or cutting from 200 or 300 yards away. Given that we were the only hunters on carefully controlled private property, we probably would have tried gobbling at the birds. That, and simulated gobbler fights, would have given us much better chances at bringing a tom into shotgun range.

Gobbler fights are not difficult to simulate. The gobblers engage in a deep, raspy kind of purr, or rattle, often called the fighting purr. They flog each other repeatedly, and the whole encounter is fairly noisy. It can bring gobblers (or hens) on the run any time, but is most effective earlier in the season when the birds are still establishing dominance. Just as rattling antlers for deer can sometimes scare off all but the most dominant bucks, the fighting purr can sometimes frighten gobblers away. For that reason, I'm inclined to use it sparingly, and usually only after trying other methods. It is a useful tactic, though, that sometimes works when nothing else will, and when it works it tends to work dramatically, often bringing in fired-up gobblers on the run.

Deer hunters will tell you that the best chances for taking a trophy buck occur during the phase of the rut when the bucks are seeking does, but the does are not yet responding. Often referred to as the "chase phase," bucks seem to throw caution to the wind during this period, traveling widely, and are vulnerable to grunting and rattling.

This, too, has its analog in turkey hunting. As the days lengthen and hormone levels rise, the gobblers become increasingly ardent in their pursuit of hens, often gobbling throughout the day. They are easy to locate, easy to keep tabs on, and vulnerable to any call that vaguely resembles any sound a hen might make. They're still wild turkeys, mind you, and extremely wary, but they definitely have a chink in their armor.

When does become responsive to bucks, the bucks seem to disappear from the woods. The wide traveling, the scraping and rubbing activity, the fighting, and the chasing of does that made them so vulnerable before suddenly comes to a near-halt. In a similar way, when the hens respond to the gobblers, the behaviors that made toms so vulnerable suddenly come to a standstill. When this happens, hunters say they are "henned up."

Hunting Henned-Up Gobblers

The lack of responsiveness Jay Novacek and I encountered in Nebraska was unusual. On the other hand, the lull between peak gobbling periods that occurs when gobblers are with hens is a problem faced frequently by turkey hunters everywhere.

Hunters are quick to claim that gobblers are "henned up." It's a convenient excuse; I've used it myself a few times. Anytime a gobbler comes off the roost and wanders off gobbling in another direction, completely ignoring our come-hither tree calls, our most seductive little yelps, and finally our exasperated cutting, we're inclined to blame hens. The fact is, gobblers generally go where they are going to go and hens, real or imitation, don't always have a lot of influence over them.

Visual sightings almost always provide useful information. Are hens with the gobbler? Does the gobbler respond in kind to challenging gobbles, or drop out of strut and slip away? Are there subordinate gobblers with the boss, and do they gobble or remain silent? Knowing these things helps the hunter develop effective strategies.

17

How do you know when gobblers are truly henned up? Often you can hear hens on the roost near a gobbler, yelping and clucking every time he gobbles. Sometimes you can see hens heading in a very obvious and determined way toward a gobbler. (If the gobbler is sounding off regularly enough to reveal his location, and you spot a hen moving toward him, run her off or flush her in the opposite direction if you can. Your chances of calling in that gobbler will go way down if a hen gets to him.)

Once, while slipping past a big pasture in southeastern Indiana, I saw a black spot in the distance that prompted me to put the binoculars to my eyes. It was a big longbeard in full strut. Through the binoculars I could see him gobbling from time to time, though I couldn't hear him. He showed no response to my diaphragm call, but when I pulled out my Quaker Boy box call and scraped out some high-volume yelps, he double-gobbled about five seconds later. I continued calling at intervals and watching the gobbler until I was convinced he was not only gobbling in response to the calls, but was headed my way.

It seemed to take that gobbler forever to reach the point at which I could put down the binoculars and still see him clearly, but it was probably about forty-five minutes to an hour. He walked along slowly, stopping to strut now and then, gobbling every time I yelped on the box call. At sixty yards, he stopped to peck around for a minute. At fifty yards, he went into a strut and hardly budged for two or three minutes. At forty-five yards I beginning to ease my gun into shooting position when something off to my right caught my attention. It was a hen, and she was running fast. She darted past me and dropped into a hollow near the edge of the pasture, hopped into the field, and kept running directly at the gobbler. She ran around him in circles several times as he strutted, then hurried off to the left and into the woods, with the gobbler right behind her.

That wasn't the first time a hen had stolen my gobbler, but it was the first time I'd had a front row seat as a hen literally ran off with him. More often, the signs will be more subtle than that. If you have a gobbler sounding off and moving your way, then fading, then moving your way only to fade again, you might suspect he is with hens. If you can get a little closer and listen carefully, you'll probably hear them.

That phenomenon was first pointed out to me by two-time world turkey-calling champion Larry Norton, who makes Turkey-Tech turkey calls and guides at Alabama's famous Bent Creek Lodge. Larry and I had hunted two days in the rain, and when the sun finally came out we were optimistic we could bring in one of Bent Creek's big gobblers. It didn't take long to get a response from a gobbler and set up on him, and within minutes he was headed our way, his gobbles reverberating through the oak glade.

Then, just when I expected to spot him any moment, the decreasing volume of his gobbles revealed he was moving away. We waited, Larry yelped, and the gobbles again began to increase in volume, only to once again fade away. This happened several times, and Larry scooted over to whisper an explanation.

"He's with hens," Larry said. "He wants to come our way, but the hens won't budge, and he doesn't want to get too far away from them."

I was skeptical. "C'mon," Larry said. "We'll slip in a little closer and you'll be able to hear them." We moved thirty or forty yards closer and began calling again, and once again the gobbler started our way. This time, though, I could faintly hear several hens yelping and even cutting a little, seeming to grow increasingly agitated as the gobbler drew closer to us, until he once again turned and went back to his harem. We opted to slip away from that confrontation and return another time-which is often the best strategy, when time permits.

There are many reasons gobblers will sound off on the roost only to stop gobbling on the ground, including heavy hunting pressure, but certainly that pattern is one clue that gobblers may be henned up. Put two or more clues together - birds approaching and fading, birds gobbling on the roost then clamming up, hens yelping from the roost near gobblers, hens spotted moving in the direction of gobblers, and so forth, and it can be determined for sure that the gobblers are henned up.

Hunting henned-up gobblers is tough. Several strategies can work. Conventional strategies, for one, shouldn't be abandoned during this period. There are always lone gobblers and satellite birds eager to sneak in and steal a hen when the boss is not around. Bringing these gobblers in under these circumstances usually calls for quiet, unaggressive calling - quiet yelps, clucks, and purrs - and plenty of patience.

Sometimes it is possible to separate a gobbler from his hens, especially if you know where they are roosting. It's not unusual for hens to roost very close to the gobbler during this time, but if you spot a gobbler going to roost, and see a hen or hens going to roost at least seventy or eighty yards away, it's possible to wait until well after dark, slip between the gobbler and the hens, and flush the hens off the roost, away from the gobbler. Set up close to where the hens were roosted before daylight, make a few quiet tree yelps, then wait for the boss to get curious about where his hens are and come looking for them.

Sometimes it's even possible to locate roosting birds in the morning and accomplish the same thing, provided the hens are roosting far enough away. Whenever you move in to set up on a gobbler in the morning, listen carefully for the sound of hens yelping. Often they'll cut in on the tag end of each gobble, and you have to be alert to catch the sounds. If they're not too close to the gobbler, move in on the hens and flush them.

Many hunters advocate bringing in henned-up gobblers by challenging the dominant hen with loud yelping or cutting. If the hen responds, the gobbler will follow. In practice, I find this a very low-percentage tactic. Far more often than not, the dominant hen will simply move away from challenging calls, and the gobbler will invariably follow. And, even on those occasions when the hen does respond, she's generally out in front of the gobbler. More than one hunter using this tactic has ended up with several hens all around him as a gobbler came into range. With several or more pair of eyes watching from different directions, it's impossible to get in position for a shot. Eventually a hen sees something she doesn't like and sounds the alarm.

The best chance for calling in a henned-up gobbler, as Larry Norton explained to me on that hunt in Alabama, is to move in close to the group and call quietly. Hens that feel unthreatened are more likely to move toward the caller than those that feel challenged.

Understand that "close" in this context doesn't mean trying to stalk with gun range, which usually isn't possible and is unsafe even when it is. By "close," I'm talking about moving in close enough to be heard with low-volume calls - eighty or ninety yards, possibly a little closer if cover, terrain, and safety considerations permit.

There is, of course, the old fallback of trying to bushwack gobblers that refuse to respond to calling. Learn where they roost, where they strut, where they eat, and which trails, logging roads, or other routes they use in traveling between these places, and set up to wait them out. It requires more knowledge, more patience, and more discipline, in my opinion, than bringing them in to a call, but it certainly can be done, and is sometimes the most effective tactic.

Finally, turkey hunters have a tendency to force the issue. That is understandable in many cases. Few of us can spend as much time in the woods as we like, and many of us are limited to hunting opening day and two or three weekends subsequent to that. Still, whenever time permits, hunters should not overlook the simple tactic of slipping away to come back later. Hens often leave turkeys about midmorning, at which point the gobblers are once again free to seek companionship elsewhere-like thirty yards from the muzzle of your shotgun, if you've returned to the area and have managed to sound like an available hen turkey.

Returning later doesn't always mean later in the morning. It might mean the next day, or a week later. Patience, persistence, and versatility often pay off in working gobblers, but knowing when to slip quietly away without disturbing an uncooperative bird, as opposed to forcing the issue and risking spooking him, is the mark of a mature turkey hunter. As Hunter's Specialties pro-staffer and well-known turkey hunter Eddie Salter once said to me, "I'm not lookin' for jus' any ol' turkey. I'm lookin' for a turkey that's ready to die."

The Post-Rut

When the hens begin sitting on nests and the gobblers get lonely, they once again become vulnerable to conventional calling. If they haven't been subjected to too much hunting pressure, they can be at their most vulnerable during this period, which is why hunting is sometimes better at the end of the season than at the beginning.

In some areas, the spring breeding cycle may be winding down, and gobling activity may be tapering off for good by season's end. Don't be quick to assume this-more than once, I've had slow days near season's end that led me to believe the gobblers were done for the spring, only to go out for one last hurrah and find that the woods were ringing with gobbles and that more than one tom seemed determined to commit suicide in response to my hen yelps.

There is no denying, though, that these final days of the season can be tough. Weather is hot, bugs are out, thick foliage decreases visibility in the woods, and tall grass discourages turkeys from entering once-inviting meadows. Gobbling activity is also tapering off. Once again the turkey hunter may be forced to bushwack birds. On the positive side, the thick foliage usually makes it easier to approach turkeys without being spotted. I've had success under these conditions by glassing pastures where cattle keep the grass short. The birds weren't usually responsive to calls, but the thick foliage enabled me to move close to them. If ever it is possible to effectively and safely stalk a wild turkey, this is the situation. The best tactic is to move away from the edge of the pasture, looping around through the woods to make the final approach.

Even generally unresponsive birds will respond to a call if the caller is close enough. It may also be possible to determine the gobbler's direction of travel, and set up at a point near the field's edge. For these late-season hunts, be sure to take plenty of water and snacks, don't forget the bug dope, and plan to hunt slowly in a few choice areas, as opposed to covering a lot of ground.

It is certainly possible to walk into the woods without a clue what the birds are doing, set up on a gobbler, and call him in. Still, the hunter who knows, or can quickly determine, the behavior patterns of turkeys with reference to which stage of the breeding cycle the birds are in, can save time that would otherwise be wasted on low-percentage tactics and greatly increase the odds for success.

Tips

• When things green up, mix a camo-brown or gray hat, green-ish shirt/vest, and brown pants.

• While it's true that turkeys are accustomed to looking for danger from above, bowhunters who hunt deer kill turkeys from tree stands every fall in states where the seasons overlap. Tree stands offer no advantage in terms of concealment, but they do offer extended visibility. This can be especially useful to hunters in areas that are new to them, enabling them to observe large areas and in effect scout as they hunt.

• When at the range patterning your shotgun, occasionally take a shot left-handed -- or right-handed, if you're a lefty. Shooting a shotgun to the offside is not that difficult if you practice a little. Having that ability can be a big advantage in hunting situations. Never practice this, though, and under pressure you'll sooner or later muff a golden opportunity.

"When the buffalo are gone we will hunt mice, for we are hunters."
--Chief Joseph, Nez Perce

Chapter 3

HUNTING FUNNELS

Every whitetail hunter is familiar with the concept of funnel hunting. Some of the most successful trophy hunters rely on this technique almost to the exclusion of all others. Turkeys are not often associated with funnels, and that is a mistake. Though there are differences between the way turkeys and deer respond to funnels, turkeys are indeed funneled by natural and man-made obstacles. Turkey hunters are keenly aware that many features of the landscape will cause birds to hang up, but don't always consider the flip side of that, which is that any feature that hangs up a bird can also tip off its whereabouts and indicate the direction it will travel, or at least narrow its options.

The differences between the way deer and turkeys respond to funnels have to do with the fact that deer prefer cover over open terrain except under the cloak of darkness, while turkeys, with the exception of nesting hens, prefer areas with less cover. This makes sense when you consider that turkeys have no sense of smell to speak of, and rely heavily on their superior eyesight to keep them safe from predators.

Adult turkeys are most vulnerable when they are in or very close to areas of thick cover. While turkeys that have been hunted or are frequently alarmed by human activities may seem hesitant at times to enter open fields, they do not have the whitetail's natural aversion to fields, and generally prefer an open meadow to a thicket. It is true that in intensively farmed areas, turkeys will inhabit small isolated woodlots so long as these are connected to other woodlots by windbreaks or tree-lined creek bottoms. At the same time, turkeys do not generally seem inclined to use these connectors the way whitetails do, and a brushy fencerow that becomes a highway for white-tailed deer may be avoided by turkeys. In a similar vein, though turkeys will often take the line of least resistance, they do not seem as inclined as deer to use saddles to cross ridgetops, or to move up or down hill by making use of draws, gullies, or ravines. What will funnel turkey movement? Roads, houses, streams, steep hills and cliffs, thickets, and fences can all influence turkeys in predictable ways.

I occasionally hunt a farm in Indiana that gives up several gobblers every year, including one or two in the twenty-four to twenty-five-pound range. A woven wire fence runs for several hundred yards along one side of the property. It has two openings. One opening was created intentionally to allow vehicles and livestock through, and the other is a spot where the fence crosses a small drainage, leaving a gap underneath. Turkeys routinely move up and down the fencerow, crossing at both spots. The equivalent for a whitetail hunter would be finding a well-used trail through a narrow band of trees connecting a cornfield to a bedding area. The hunter knows that if he uses the wind properly, he will not have to wait long to see deer.

The landowner hunts the property every year, and I often join him. Neither of us is inclined to hunt the fence openings, but I can remember when the landowner was new to turkey hunting, and growing increasingly frustrated at his inability to fill his tag. Eventually, from listening to gobblers morning after morning, he figured out how they were using the fence openings, set up by one of them, and took his first gobbler: a twenty-five-pound tom with one and one-half-inch spurs. He was elated, and why not? He had put in the time to pattern the birds, then set up accordingly. And no matter how good the setup, a hunter must still spot the turkey before it spots him, remain motionless, estimate range accurately, get his gun into position without being spotted, and then get off a good shot.

Turkeys use trails and logging roads far more than deer do. If the vegetation on either side of the road is very thick, such roads are funnels in the strictest sense of the word. The intersection of two logging roads can be a real hotspot. The two roads together double the chances for seeing a turkey, and such an intersection often creates the kind of opening that gobblers like to strut in.

In a similar fashion, turkeys are often funneled along ridgetops. And in big hill country, the contours may be steep, but they are often interrupted at intervals by flat areas, or benches, running parallel to the ridgelines. Many turkeys stay high in such areas, frequenting the ridgetops and the highest benches, and rarely going to the valley below. If these benches are not too wide, and if the hillsides above and below them are fairly steep, they will tend to funnel turkey movement as surely as any trail or road.

Years ago, when I was a young turkey hunter eager to put more notches on my turkey gun, I hunted such a place. I had scouted it on only one occasion, and did not know the area well. On opening day, I was making my way east to west along the ridgetop when I heard a gobble. I set up in the semi-darkness, and the bird responded lustily to my first tentative yelps.

Though it was long ago, I recall that morning vividly. The forest had not been logged for years at the highest elevations, and I was set up in a big glade of mature oaks. When the sun came over the ridgetop the light filtered down through those giant oaks in bands that lent a soft glow to everything they touched, imparting a feeling of depth and drama to the landscape. Sixty yards out, the gobbler stepped into a shaft of light and began his performance, pirouetting slowly in full strut, his iridescent colors shimmering as he turned first this way and then another.

Despite the scene's beauty, it was a poor spot for a setup. In the predawn darkness, not being familiar with the area, I had neglected to notice a huge patch of multiflora rose that now stood between the gobbler and me, and the big tom refused to go through or around it. When he eventually wandered off, I rose slowly to my feet and pulled off my headset so I could see better.

Farming, development, and logging have robbed much of the eastern U.S. of its once spectacular natural beauty, but occasionally, usually in remote and hilly or mountainous terrain, a hunter can catch a glimpse of what it once was.

I stood for a long time in that spot before deciding to move down the ridge-line and look for a duel with another gobbler rather than try to relocate on the first. My duel with Gobbler Number Two was unsuccessful. The next day I was in the same area, this time on the right side of the multiflora rose. The gobbler sounded off from the roost on cue. Once again I was treated to a spectacular sunrise in that oak glade, but this time the gobbler headed off down the ridge in the other direction, gobbling in response to my plaintive yelps, but refusing to come my way.

A little later that morning I discovered what I was sure was his roosting spot, and came up with a strategy I was confident would enable me to bag him, if only he roosted there a third time. A spur or secondary point sloped gently away for about eighty yards to the south of the main ridgeline, where it ended in a steep bluff looking out over the valley. Given my earlier setup locations and the directions from which the gobbling on the roost came, I was sure the bird was roosting in a big oak near the end of that point. I was also sure that when he came off the roost, he walked up that spur to the main ridge, then moved east or west along the ridgetop.

Next morning, well before first light, I made my way to the spot where the spur intersected with the main ridge. I didn't use a diaphragm call back then, only box calls and slates. It didn't matter; I didn't even take a call from my pocket. I listened to the bird gobble on the roost for what seemed like forever. I heard him fly down. Ten minutes later I spotted him slipping like a ghost through the trees and up the slight incline where the spur joined the main ridge. He passed by to my right, making for an awkward shot, but when he went behind a cluster of junipers about thirty yards away I shifted the gun to my left shoulder. When he cleared the evergreens I pulled the trigger. Twenty-one and one-half pounds, eleven-inch beard, one and a quarter-inch spurs. Yes, I ambushed him, though I don't think that occurred to me as I carried him back through that beautiful oak glade and down off that long, steep hill.

The intersection of two meadows, pastures, or cropfields can tend to funnel turkeys. On fact, there is just such a spot on my Ohio hunting lease. An old pasture, more than fifty acres, runs roughly east and west on high ground. A much smaller opening of about two acres adjoins the main pasture, entering it at right angles from the north. Several redbud trees extend partway across the intersection, providing great cover and further funneling any birds going from one part of the pasture to the other. That spot is a favorite strut zone. I like to put a blind there and save the spot for those times when I take youngsters or beginning turkey hunters afield. It's a rare day that we don't at least see a few turkeys from that spot.

Another hotspot on that same field is near the east end, where a logging road comes up the hill and enters from the north. Across from the road entrance a small, overgrown drainage extends about forty yards into the field from the south, creating a choke point that puts any bird moving through it in easy shotgun range. The result is an intersection where birds moving east or west in the pasture are forced into range, at a precise spot where turkeys also enter the pasture on the logging road. That area can be counted on to give up one or two gobblers every spring.

On numerous occasions I've bagged gobblers on haul roads, ridgetop trails, fencelines, or openings between fields. Whether they came in strutting and gobbling, or pecked along feeding as they walked, or sneaked toward me as if the boss gobbler had just caught them with a hen, I always wondered the same thing: Did that bird come my way in response to my calling, or was it just headed my way and I was in the right spot at the right time? It's not a question that tortures my soul: I just want to know whether to give myself credit for my calling skills, or for my expertise in selecting a setup!

"A turkey is more occult and awful than all the angels and archangels. Insofar as God has partly revealed to us an angelic world, he has partly told us what an angel means. But God has never told us what a turkey means. And if you go and stare at a live turkey for an hour or two, you will find by the end of it that the enigma has rather increased than diminished."

--G.K. Chesterton
All Things Considered, "Christmas" 1908

Chapter 4

THE PERFECT SETUP

Ever hike to the top of a ridge, only to hear a gobbler sounding off on the other ridge, across the valley? You try everything to get a tom to sound off on your ridge, but nothing doing. So down the mountain you go, across the valley, through the creek, and up the other mountain to the ridgetop. The gobbler is long-gone, or at least silent now, but right on cue a gobbler sounds off from the ridgetop you just left.

Finding the perfect setup is a lot like that. It looks good until you sit down, then the foliage is too thick, or the spot is too exposed, or you can't see into the creek bottom, or an unavoidable knot in the tree digs into your back so there is no way you can sit still if a gobbler approaches. Unless a turkey is very close, I rarely drop into a spot and just stay there. It probably speaks more to my compulsiveness than anything else, but when I move in to set up on a gobbler, I usually scramble around to try three or four spots before resigning myself to one; I often end up in the first spot I tried.

The perfect setup may be illusory, but selecting a good setup is important, and greatly influences our odds of bringing a bird into range and getting a good shot at him. There are several characteristics of a good setup about which all turkey hunters can agree: It should involve a tree wide enough to provide some safety from behind; it should be comfortable enough to enable the hunter to sit reasonably still for long periods of time; it should not restrict the direction in which the hunter can shoot; and it should permit adequate visibility and range. Beyond these, there are two basic schools of thought about what constitutes a desirable setup.

Note how well the part of this hunter in the shade is well hidden, and how visible the part in sunlight. Whether sitting or moving, seek shade when possible.

Two Setups: Hi-Vis vs. Maximum Concealment

No doubt every turkey hunter remembers his first turkey. I remember mine as vividly as if it were yesterday, and in taking that first gobbler I instinctively selected a setup that illustrates one of the two schools of thought.

When the gobbler sounded off from a hilltop about 150 yards away, I quickly looked around for a place to set up. I was standing on another hilltop, in a stand of thick, second-growth timber. I made my way quickly off to my right, into a more open section of the woods, sat down, and scratched out a few yelps on my box call. The gobbler thundered back, heading into the valley between us. I wasn't satisfied with where I was sitting. If the gobbler continued to come directly toward me, he would crest the hill and be visible about fifty-five or sixty yards out. I scampered forward to sit against another tree, this one about forty yards from the lip of the hill. Soon I could hear the gobbler walking in the dry oak leaves, and was able to track him precisely by the sound. When his white head emerged over the lip of the hill like a periscope, the front bead of my Ithaca was on it and I pulled the trigger. He weighed twenty-one and one-half pounds, had an eleven-inch beard, and one-inch spurs -- I was elated.

More to the point, I had hit on an approach to setting up on turkeys that I continued to use, whenever possible, for years after that. Not that I invented it, mind you. It's really just a common-sense approach used by many hunters. The idea motivating the approach is as simple as "If you can't see him, he can't see you." Many hunters prefer to find a setup that puts the turkey in range the moment he comes into view. The maximum effective range on my old Ithaca was forty yards, so I felt most comfortable setting up that many yards from the lip of that hill. Hills are the simplest application of that principle, but it can just as easily be a bend in a logging road, an inside corner of a meadow, or a screen of trees. The turkey's eyes are its number one defense, and this kind of setup takes them out of the picture. A lot of gobblers have been bowled over the instant they crested a hill, walked around a bend in a logging road, or emerged into the open from a screen of trees.

This approach works particularly well when a fired-up gobbler comes in gobbling, enabling the hunter to track its progress and wait in preparation. It does have its weaknesses, though. Gobblers don't always announce their progress with conveniently spaced gobbles. Sometimes they sneak in all the way. Sometimes they come in gobbling but hang up. Sometimes they gobble partway in, than clam up when they get close. When this happens, the hunter is often caught flat-footed as the gobbler steps into range at, say, the two o'clock position. And how many of us have given up on a turkey and stood to leave the area, or tried to relocate on the gobbler, only to see or hear the bird run off or flush. The knowledge that if only you had waited one or two minutes more and you'd have had the gobbler in your lap is disheartening.

Pinned down. It happens to every turkey hunter. Only option here in most cases is to freeze until the bird steps behind a large tree, rock or thick cover, then get quickly in position and wait.

Hunters opting for this sort of setup should keep in mind that gobblers tend to come in from unexpected directions. A spot in which visibility or shooting lanes are limited to one or two directions is probably not a good spot. I relearned that lesson several years ago when my friend and fellow outdoor writer Tony Mandile drove from Phoenix to hunt Eastern turkeys with me in south-central Ohio. On opening morning I led Tony to a hillside from which I often heard gobblers on the roost, and right on cue they sounded off. I set up about thirty yards behind Tony, and began calling at first light. It wasn't long before Tony signaled to me that he saw a gobbler. It wasn't one gobbler, as it turned out, but eleven of them, in a single flock! We should not have seen eleven gobblers in a flock in southern Ohio at that time of year, but there they were. They were a loud bunch, too. A roving brawl is what it was, as the flock moved through the woods, two of them in particular flogging away at each other. They came down the hillside opposite us, across the creek, and straight up the hill as if they were going to walk over us.

There seemed to be birds everywhere. I put the bead on one, waiting for Tony to shoot. I was the host, and he had come all the way from Phoenix, so I wasn't going to shoot a bird that would ruin his opportunity, though he later insisted I should have shot. I waited for Tony to shoot, and waited. It never happened. Eventually, the roving brawl moved away from us, and we lowered our guns.

The problem, in part, was that Tony couldn't get a clear shot at one bird. But the problem was also that a large deadfall, a hollow in the ground, and some high weeds behind us, blocked several of Tony's shot opportunities. It was a poor setup. A few years of hunting that spot had led me to expect that roosting turkeys would fly down and then walk the trail from the east, along the side of the hill we were sitting on, presenting an easy shot. Instead, these birds hadn't used the trail, but had looped to the south and come in from that direction. Had I set Tony up twenty yards away in either direction, he'd have filled his tag. Never expect a gobbler to appear from the obvious direction, and you'll be right more often than not.

There's a turkey out there somewhere. Some concealment helps hide a hunter's movements, but too much makes spotting the turkey and getting a clean shot all but impossible.

Clearly, there are advantages to being able to see a gobbler at longer distances, and that is the principle behind the second school on setting up properly. Champion Caller and Bent Creek Lodge guide Larry Norton is a proponent of that approach.

"I like to be able to see that gobbler as far away as I can," Larry told me years ago. "I want to know how he is reacting to my calls. If I can see what he's doing, I know when to call more, when to call less, or when to stop calling. If he hangs up, I know it. If he's got hens with him, I can see them. If he wanders off, I can see which way he's going and move to head him off, instead of sitting in the same spot calling for another half an hour to a bird that's not there."

As far as being spotted by the gobbler, Larry is confident that his camouflage will provide adequate concealment, so long as he sits motionless. A hunt in Tennessee illustrated for me the advantages of visibility in turkey hunting. I eased through a saddle in a hilltop to set up on a gobbler that seemed determined to shake the leaves off the trees with his booming gobbles. As soon as I cleared the saddle, though, I could hear my hunting partner Dan yelping away on his box call. I couldn't see Dan, but I could tell he was up a drainage across the small valley I was looking down on. I had a ringside seat, and didn't have to wait long to see the big gobbler making its way down the valley toward Dan. After that, though, things slowed down considerably. The tom was gobbling and double gobbling every time Dan yelped, which naturally encouraged him to really pour it on. The problem was that every time he yelped, the gobbler stopped to strut. It would come out of its strut and take five or ten steps toward Dan, then he would yelp and the gobbler would stop, go into full strut, and pirhouette around for awhile. Dan would yelp, the tom would gobble and double gobble. Whenever Dan stopped yelping for twenty seconds or so, the bird would begin walking toward him, but it would never get more than a few steps before Dan would yelp, forcing the tom to stop again and strut for awhile. It was almost agonizing to watch this, but it was enlightening. No doubt I had done the same thing myself before, without realizing it. When a gobbler gets fired up, the caller naturally tends to keep calling aggressively, but I could see now that that can be a mistake.

It was a relief when Dan pulled the trigger on that bird, almost an hour and a half later. I suspect he could have filled his tag in fifteen minutes had he not called so frequently. The problem was, he couldn't see the gobbler, so he didn't know that his calling was slowing down the bird's approach. Am I saying that I've settled on the high-visibility approach to setting up on turkeys? Not exactly. After years of turkey hunting, there are still a few issues I haven't resolved, and this is one of them.

Sometimes, of course, the situation is out of the hunter's hands. A bird gobbles from over a bank fifteen yards away, and there is nothing to do but drop to the ground and get the gun up. In some hilly, second-growth forests, broad vistas are not an option, while in mountains or plains, they are the only option.

There is often some choice in the matter, though. If a gobbler is sounding off regularly and seems fired up, I usually opt for a setup that will have the bird in range when I see him. Otherwise, I usually opt for maximum visibility. And of course, whichever option I go for, I often wish I'd gone the other route.

If one or the other approach appeals strongly to you, it's probably the right one for you. The hunter who worries that movement will give him away will do well to limit visibility. The hunter who is confident that his camouflage and ability to sit motionless for long periods will provide adequate concealment should take advantage of that confidence and seek maximum visibility.

This bowhunter's chances of getting to full draw without being spotted are extremely low. Some sort of concealment, whether a prepared blind or good natural cover, is mandatory in bowhunting turkeys.

Regardless of the approach you use, it is usually worth taking the time to select a setup carefully. We tend to move hastily when a gobbler responds to our call, but we usually have more time than we think we do. Pick the right spot, and get comfortable. If you're not comfortable initially, you're not going to get any more comfortable over time - move to a better spot, now! Comfort is the key to sitting still and to sticking it out if the bird takes his time coming in.

Home Improvements

If there is a common turkey hunting accessory that is highly underused, it would have to be pruning shears. At times they are all but indispensable. With pruning shears a hunter can move obstructions that would prevent shooting in a given direction, or at all. He can move weeds or other growth that limit visibility. At the same time, a few limbs cut and stuck in the ground in strategic places can do a lot to break up a hunter's outline and provide some concealment. Don't make the mistake of thinking a thin screen of limbs will conceal movement, because it won't. But it will make a hunter less exposed, and provide an important margin of protection against the eagle eyes of a turkey.

Tips

• Aggressive run and gun tactics are exciting and productive, but usually net two-year-old birds. If you're after a real trophy, low-key calling while sitting in a blind near favored strutting zones is a very effective tactic.

• When it's time to move on a hung-up tom, wait for a gobble that will reveal his location. Try a hen call or a locator call if the bird isn't gobbling spontaneously. When you get the gobble, you'll have a much better idea of whether or not it's safe to move.

• In excellent turkey habitat, the spring home range of turkeys will usually be less than 300 acres. That means that in good turkey country, there is almost always at least one turkey within hearing range of your call. Hunting with that in mind will boost your success rate.

"Th' real old hunter uses what they call a lion's tongue. Cuts 'em in half an' lets 'em wilt and puts 'em in their mouth, and they just make a hen ashamed of itself."

--Grady Waldroop,
as quoted in *The Foxfire Book*, 1972

Chapter 5

ADVANCED CALLING STRATEGIES

Can we lay to rest the myth of the turkey-calling champions who impress judges but can't fool real turkeys? Somewhere there may be such a caller, and it is certainly true that there is a big difference between contest calling and hunting. The thing is, I've had the good fortune to hunt with a number of turkey-calling champions; every one of them was keenly aware of the difference between contest calling and hunting, and every one of them was an excellent turkey hunter. It is, after all, a passion for turkey hunting that usually fuels the inspiration to take up contest calling in the first place.

The endless debate about the relative importance of calling skills is really a complex issue. Most calling champions will tell you that calling skills are not the most important attribute of a good turkey hunter. Some of them are sincere and some, I suspect, are just being modest. At the risk of sounding like a politician, I would argue that the relative importance of calling skills depends in part on how we define "calling skills."

If by "calling skills" we mean the ability to precisely imitate the various sounds of a live turkey, I agree with others that this ability is of secondary importance at best. On some days it seems that gobblers will respond to any sound that vaguely resembles a hen yelp. My daughter, at age nine, once called in a pair of longbeards using a Quaker Boy push-pin box call after about one minute of coaching in the car on the way to the hunt.

Meanwhile, the world-calling champions I have hunted with have demonstrated time and again that there are many days on which even world-class calling will not seduce a wily tom turkey. On the other hand, if our definition of "calling

35

skills" includes knowing when to call and when not to, when to use which calls, when to call loudly and aggressively and when to call quietly, how to use various "non-vocal" sounds that turkeys make to bring in gobblers, then I would have to argue that calling skills are very important. Yes, you can bag plenty of gobblers by yelping on a box call, without resorting to calls other than a plain yelp, and without ever mastering a different style of call. Over the long run you'll bag more gobblers, though, if you expand your calling to include more variety.

Box calls have earned a place in every serious turkey hunter's vest. Their downside is the movement required to operate them, which can often be hidden with natural color, a blind, or a piece of camo fabric over the knees.

Improving Sound Quality

We'll start with this because it is probably the least important. Accurately mimicking the sound of a turkey builds confidence, though, and confidence is important. Beginning callers often make two mistakes: they use tapes exclusively as a source of learning, and they practice indoors.

Audio and video tapes are excellent tools to help you learn how to call turkeys, and they are getting better all the time. The best ones feature the recorded sounds of live turkeys, or a mix of live turkeys and expert callers. Even for the experienced caller, tapes can be great refreshers after not calling for many months, especially in learning the cadence and the dynamics of turkey calls. The best sound system, though, is no match for the real thing. Beyond a certain point, calling will not improve until the caller spends time in the woods listening to real, live turkeys.

Most callers at some point have experienced the following. They practice for hours at home or in their vehicles and are increasingly satisfied with their calling. Then, on opening day they begin calling in the woods, and find themselves examining their call to see if it's defective. The sound in the open woods is altogether different than the sound at home or in a vehicle. There is much more reverberation indoors, and calls outdoors may seem flat and lifeless by comparison. It's important to spend some time practicing outdoors. Dedicated callers take a tape recorder outside, put it at some distance from themselves, and record their calling to analyze it later and find ways to improve.

Most box calls should be tuned. Mark the screw on the "lid" and try it at different settings, stopping when it elicits regular responses.

Mastering Various Types of Calling Devices

Assuming the other basic woodsmanship skills are in place, this may be the simplest thing a hunter can do to boost his success rate. For reasons known only to turkeys, a given gobbler on a given day will respond only to a box call, not to a diaphragm call. Or maybe it's a slate call that suddenly inspires him to drop out of a full strut and run 200 yards for a rendezvous with a load of copper-coated No. 6s. Some hunters will not enter the woods without their trusty boat-paddle-style box call because there have been times when it elicited gobbles and nothing else would.

Hunters often believe a certain call is successful because the turkeys in that area have never heard it before. This is why some hunters swear by tube calls or wing-bone calls, which are far less common than box calls and diaphragm calls. There is some evidence of late that turkeys respond best to sounds that are above the range of human hearing, and several manufacturers are now marketing calls which work at that level.

Since we can't get inside a turkey's peanut-sized brain to see what is going on there, we'll never be sure of the motivation. It does seem clear, though, that turkeys can be finicky about which sound they'll respond to. That being the case, it is to the hunter's advantage to master at least several different styles of calls and carry them with him whenever he hunts.

Some are more difficult to master than are others, but any hunter can carry one or two box calls, including a pin-push style, and one or two slate-type friction calls. Wing-bone and tube calls are among the most difficult to master, but they offer the aforementioned advantage of being less frequently heard in the turkey woods.

Diaphragm calls are less difficult to learn than tube or wing-bone calls, though not as easy to learn as friction calls. There are very successful turkey hunters who don't use diaphragm calls, but they do offer several advantages, and every turkey hunter should give them a try. They're small and light, and that makes for a lot of versatility. You can carry a dozen of them in a small container, and no two of them will sound alike. They'll emulate sounds ranging from that of a young, sweet hen, to that of the raspiest old hen in the flock. They'll produce fly-down cackles, purrs, cuts, and yelps.

Perhaps their biggest advantage is that they enable the hunter to call without moving. There are times when a cluck or a few soft purrs will persuade a wary gobbler standing in full view sixty yards away to move in. The hunter with a friction call may be pinned down, unable to move his hands without being spotted, but the hunter with a mouth call can purr away while remaining motionless. And who knows how many gobblers sneaking in silently from an unexpected direction have melted away into the forest upon spotting the hand movements of a hunter working a friction call?

Clearly, there is no one style of call that is essential for turkey hunting success, but the hunter who learns to use a wider variety of calls will be a more versatile, and hence better, hunter.

Non-Vocal Calls

These consist of scratching in the leaves, drumming, and flapping wings. I have heard some hunters talk about fooling turkeys by scraping wings against trees, but I've never heard a turkey do that, and I have not tried it. There is another sound I have heard turkeys make that I have never heard emulated, and that is a kind of rattling sound some gobblers make with their wings, and possibly their tails, while strutting. It sounds like gravel being shaken in a shoebox.

Most hunters have at one time or another been walking through dry leaves only to have a gobbler sound off from very close by. Sometimes gobblers mistake a hunter walking slowly through dry leaves for a turkey walking, which is not surprising, especially if the person stops now and then and changes pace. There have been times when I was sure an approaching turkey was a hunter. It only makes sense, when moving through dry leaves is unavoidable, to walk with a slow, irregular cadence.

Scratching in the leaves is even easier. Turkeys often follow a peculiar scratch, scratch-scratch, scratch cadence when digging after acorns or other foods under the leaves. They scratch first with one foot, then make two quick scratches with the other foot, then scratch again with the first foot. It's easy to imitate, and often fools turkeys. I don't recommend starting with this call, or even using it randomly, since it may put turkeys on the alert. It's a good one to try now and then, though, when a turkey is hung up close by and doesn't seem to be responding to calling. Drumming is probably the most interesting sound turkeys make. Sometimes toms that do not gobble at all will nonetheless strut and drum. The theory is that these are subordinate birds, reluctant to gobble for fear of getting a good flogging from the local boss. Drumming is a way to more quietly advertise for hens. If this is accurate, it is easy to see why drumming can be effective, at least for bringing in a dominant bird. Drumming doesn't always work, of course - anything that always worked would have to be illegal. It is a good ploy to try when other tactics fail to produce. Several manufacturers are now marketing calls that simulate drumming gobblers.

The sound of turkey wings flapping is a common one in the turkey woods, heard when turkeys fly down from the roost, fly up to the roost, or when they fight. There are devices marketed to create this sound, and some hunters carry real turkey wings to do it. For my own part, I'm not convinced that the old technique of yanking a camo handkerchief rapidly taut and loose with both hands doesn't do as adequate a job, and I have brought a few turkeys in after doing this, though I have never done it without also making a fly-down cackle and, in most cases, a few quiet yelps. I'm told that in the case of call-shy old solitary gobblers, the flapping sounds of a bird flying off the roost, to the exclusion of all other sounds, can sometimes be effective. I don't doubt it, but can't speak to that from personal experience.

When to Call Aggressively, Quietly, or Not at All

Years ago, when I first had the opportunity to hunt with some of the better-known turkey hunting experts, it was a real confidence builder to spend a day in the woods with them and return empty-handed. That might sound strange, but hunting with these famous turkey hunters and seeing that they did not always succeed was reassuring. They hunted with a confidence that was born not of a feeling that they were sure to bag a gobbler every time out, but with the knowledge that sooner or later their tactics would work.

I was curious to observe their hunting styles, to see who hunted aggressively and covered a lot of ground, who relied more on discipline and patience, who called loudly and often, who exercised more restraint in calling. Certainly there were differences in hunting styles, but what I found over time was that most of them were difficult to pigeonhole. Depending on where they were hunting and how the birds were responding, they changed their tactics, sometimes prospecting and covering a lot of ground, sometimes setting up in a likely spot and waiting out birds, sometimes cackling and cutting and lost yelping, sometimes calling only with an occasional cluck or a little purring.

A gobbler approaching silently will often stop and cluck. If he hears a cluck in return, he is reassured and comes in. If not, he slips away.

How did they know which strategy to use? They didn't. If they "knew,"we'd have killed turkeys every time we hunted. They made educated guesses, based on experience, and they experimented. Sometimes, it seemed, anything would work, and other times nothing would. Over time, though, the hunter who is versatile, adaptable, uses his best judgment, and is not afraid to experiment, will take more turkeys than the hunter who always uses the same strategy, no matter what the birds are doing.

There is a greater degree of consensus about how best to approach some situations than others. Here are a few calling strategies about which most experienced turkey hunters can agree.

First, if a gobbler indicates by his reaction that he likes a certain call, keep giving it to him. If loud yelps from a box call have him double-gobbling and moving pretty quickly in your direction, keep giving him loud yelps from a box call.

Most hunters will agree that as the bird moves closer, it's usually smart to back off on the volume and frequency of calls. Turkeys have an amazing ability to determine exactly where a sound is coming from for some distance. When you're working a bird into range, you want him hunting for you, not looking right at you. If the bird knows your precise location, you run the risk that 1) he will be expecting to see a hen there, and may hang up or even slip away if he doesn't, and 2) he will see you.

Loud and aggressive calling has its place, but rarely if ever will that be when a gobbler is on the roost. To begin with, hens rarely call aggressively from the roost. Then too, a gobbler that hears a hen yelping aggressively is expecting that hen to come to him under the roost. Often a gobbler will continue to strut on the roost, pausing occasionally to peek at the forest floor for the hen he knows is approaching, as long as a hunter continues calling. Only when the calling stops for a period of time will the gobbler fly down. For this reason, a few quiet tree yelps are adequate until the gobbler flies down. A fly-down cackle is about as aggressive as a hunter would normally want to be when calling to a roosted bird.

The exception to that might be if you know you are competing with real hens roosted nearby. Then you might try pouring it on. It's a long shot, but probably as likely to succeed as anything under those circumstances.

Toms that seem call-shy, either because they are subordinate birds or because they have been subjected to a lot of hunting pressure, are more likely to respond to quiet, infrequent calling than to loud, aggressive calling. In a similar vein, call-shy gobblers are unlikely to respond to gobbles, to drumming, or to fighting purrs.

The closer you get to a gobbler, the more likely he will respond to your calls. Keep in mind, though, that safety is a major concern here. Apart from that, moving in close to a gobbler risks spooking him, ruining the hunt for that morning, and possibly educating that bird and making him tougher for the rest of the season. When safety concerns are satisfied, and when hilly terrain, thick foliage, and a certainty of the gobbler's location permit it, hunters can sometimes slip to within sixty yards or so of a gobbler. From that location, a cluck or a few quiet yelps will often generate a quick response in a gobbler that paid no attention to calls from more typical distances of 150 yards or more.

Experts often talk of taking a gobbler's temperature, by which they mean determining how fired up and eager the bird seems to be by calling with increasing aggressiveness. If aggressive calling results in more frequent gobbling, double and triple gobbling, and a bird moving steadily if not rapidly toward the hunter, then the callers continues with aggressive calling as long as the bird continues to respond and come in, backing off only as the gobbler gets closer. On the other hand, if the gobbler does not increase gobbling frequency in response to more aggressive calling, it's time to back off, calling less frequently and with less volume.

Is there a time not to call at all? Occasionally you will encounter a gobbler so call shy he is almost impossible to bring in, even with the most non-aggressive calling. One option is to seek a more cooperative gobbler - a smart option in many cases. But if he happens to be a long-spurred old gobbler, or if he manages to get under your skin and you want that particular bird, your only real option is to hunt with minimal calling, or none at all.

You might try a very infrequent, very quiet yelp, or just a cluck. Or you might try setting up to bushwhack the bird, without calling at all. It requires extreme discipline and patience, and there is no guarantee of success, but it can work.

The bottom line on all this is that most experienced turkey hunters these days vary their calling in terms of frequency and volume, letting the birds themselves indicate which kind of calling they prefer on a given day.

Additional Techniques and Tips

We've looked at moving in close to a gobbler when conditions permit. The opposite can work, too. When two or more hunters work together, they can sometimes employ what is variously called the "ghost hen," the "floating hen," or the "fading hen." If a gobbler seems hung up, one caller slips away very quietly and calls from different positions farther and farther behind the hunter. The idea is that when the gobbler thinks his hen is moving away from him, he'll pursue, and this will bring him past the shooter, within range.

This is an effective technique that has put a lot of gobblers on the dinner table. Three caveats: first, moving as a gobbler is approaching is always risky. You want to be sure you are not visible to the bird. If he spots movement, that duel is probably over. Second, this method works best when you know the area well. If an obstacle such as a stream, thicket, or fence is hanging up the bird, success is unlikely. And finally, this is an approach to be used only after you're reasonably sure the bird is hung up, and you've already tried a few other approaches to get him off the spot. The reason for this is that whenever the caller separates himself from the designated shooter, there is a risk that another gobbler will approach from a different direction, out of range of the shooter. It's even possible that the original gobbler will move past the shooter without providing a shot, either because he is just out of range, or because a thicket or obstacles of some sort make a clear shot impossible.

One tactic that is probably not used often enough is the silent treatment. When a bird gobbles in response to calls but seems to hang up or go silent, try putting the call aside and waiting him out. Give him at least twenty minutes. Often he'll come sneaking in to see where his hen went.

A couple of final tips:

Clucks can be among the most effective calls. A single, isolated cluck seems to mean "I'm over here, where are you?" I believe that in many cases a hung-up gobbler will remain silent for a while, then cluck one time. If he gets a cluck in response, he is reassured and comes in. If not, he slips away. Stay alert for that single cluck. When you hear it, cluck back and get your gun in position.

Many hunters don't use locator calls, complaining that they rarely work. It is true that locators don't always elicit gobbles. Stick with them, though, and use them regularly, and they will work on occasion. Unless a hunter is seated with his gun in position, it is always better to elicit a gobble with a locator call than with a turkey call. This causes the gobbler to reveal his position without moving toward the hunter. Every turkey hunter occasionally has this experience: he is working his way along a ridgetop trail or a logging road, stopping to yelp occasionally. He walks over a rise and around a bend only to catch a glimpse of a gobbler flushing or ducking into the woods. It's possible, of course, that the gobbler just happened to be there. But more than likely, the gobbler heard the approaching "hen" and was headed for a rendezvous with her. Had the hunter been able to elicit a shock gobble, he'd have been set up and ready. And even if he hadn't, the gobbler would not have been moving toward him and there would have been less chance of spooking it.

In a variation of that theme, the hunter stops and yelps, only to have a gobbler sound off from over a bank or on the other side of a thicket. Before the hunter can finish yanking on his headnet and scampering into position, the bird has peeked over the bank or around the thicket and spotted his frantic activity.

Certainly there are many times when a gobbler will gobble in response to a turkey call, but not to a locator call. That's why, when the locator doesn't work, we reach for the turkey call. It's always worth trying the locator first, though. When you decide to yelp loudly as a locator, better to do it where visibility is good, and in a spot that will allow you to drop and get in position quickly.

Which locator is the best? Every experienced turkey hunter has his favorite. I sometimes use an owl call, especially early in the morning, but generally prefer something louder. Crow calls work for me on occasion, but in areas where there are crows squawking nonstop, I reach for something else. Any loud sound can work, even air horns.

Pileated woodpecker calls can be effective. One morning, digging around in my gear still more asleep than awake, I put a goose call in my vest pocket by mistake. I used it, just for laughs, and it worked!

Gobblers may respond to any loud, sudden noise. Sometimes less commonly heard sounds, such as the goose call, work best.

Locators are typically used to find a gobbler when prospecting, but they can be useful at getting a tom to reveal his location any time. If you've worked a bird in close, and he suddenly clams up on you for ten minutes or so, slip a locator out and give a blast on it. If the bird is close by, he will usually gobble in response to a loud locator.

Sometimes it is necessary to relocate on a gobbler. That is always a tricky maneuver. Every effort should be made to get the gobbler to sound off and reveal his location before moving, or you risk spooking the bird. Once you hear him gobble and determine his position, you can move safely and with a better idea where to go. Pull out all the calling stops if necessary. Cluck, to see if the bird is in close. Yelp, softly a time or two, and then with increasing volume and frequency. Try cutting, then use the locator. Only as a last resort should you attempt to relocate without getting a gobble from the bird.

Gobbling is a controversial call, mostly because of safety concerns. It's probably not a good idea on public land, unless the area is remote and you are confident there aren't other hunters in the area. Even on private land, gobbling is something to undertake with caution. The situation in which I most often use gobbling is when I'm roosting a bird in an area where afternoon hunting is prohibited. Occasionally, when I'm hunting private land, and am set up in a spot from which I have good visibility and would easily see any nearby hunters, I will gobble to locate a bird. A gobble is more likely to send toms running off than to bring them in, but it can be effective on dominant birds. It should be used sparingly, and with an extra measure of caution.

There is a wide range of calling skills, and calling styles, among the best turkey hunters. Most of the more consistently successful callers have these attributes in common, though: Versatility, in terms of being able to use at least several different kinds of calls; confidence that their calling will sooner or later bring in a gobbler; and a willingness to experiment, to try different calling tactics until they hit on the right one to bring a given gobbler on a given day to the gun.

"If he answers y' when y'yelp to'im, an' he gobbles as much as twice, why, y'can be assured if y'don't get'im excited he'll come right t'that spot. But y'can almost bat'ch-er eye an' 'fut!' he's gone."

--Jake Waldroop
from a quote in The Foxfire Book

Chapter 6

BLINDS

I've become convinced in recent years that the majority of turkey hunters could tag more birds if they hunted from blinds. Does that mean I think every turkey hunter should run out, buy a blind, and use it religiously? Not at all. There is far more to turkey hunting than killing more birds, and hunting from a blind is a style of hunting that won't appeal to everyone. At the same time, blinds offer more advantages than might come readily to mind, and merit serious consideration.

Not too many years ago, I considered blinds an evil necessity to be used only when photographing turkeys or bowhunting. I resented lugging them around, I hated taking the time to set them up and take them down, and I chafed at the way they limited my mobility, convinced I could bag that gobbler that had been hammering back at my hen yelps for an hour if only I were unencumbered by the blind. Two things changed my mind. First, it gradually became apparent that (assuming I was hunting an area I knew) I saw more gobblers when I was in the blind than when I was not. Following hot gobblers through the woods, playing various cat and mouse games, is a fun, exciting, and sometimes productive way to hunt, but the notion that mobility will put hunters in shotgun range more often than staying put in a good spot is largely an illusion.

Second, blinds themselves changed. There are now available blinds that are so light and so compact, and which go up and down so quickly, that they hardly limit mobility at all. There is still a niche in turkey hunting for the older-style, less-portable blinds, but the new ones are so good, and so effective, that using them almost feels like cheating.

**Up close and personal. Blinds can put even kids and beginners
close to turkeys for hunting, observation, or photography.**

Who Needs Them?

I rarely use blinds when I'm hunting alone with a firearm. I do find them useful in certain situations, however. You might give serious consideration to a blind if:

1) You are a bowhunter.
2) You sometimes take youngsters or less experienced hunters turkey hunting.
3) You sometimes like to turkey hunt with a companion.
4) You are unable to sit still for long periods, either because of a bad back, an injury, or a naturally busy disposition.
5) You enjoy photographing turkeys, or observing them at close range for long periods.

In the chapters devoted to bowhunting and guiding I've discussed the use of blinds for bowhunters, youngsters, and less experienced hunters.

Even if none of the above applies to you, I believe there are situations in which every turkey hunter can benefit greatly from a blind. We'll get to those situations shortly, but first let's look at items 3 to 5. I believe that turkey hunting should usually be a solitary activity. Normally, when I hunt with a companion or two, we wish one another good luck and then split up to hunt different areas. Not every turkey hunters prefers to hunt solo, though. Blinds, assuming they are large enough, are probably the most effective way for two people to hunt together. Though two experienced hunters together can sometimes employ strategies that are effective on gobblers, as a rule it is four times as difficult for two hunters to bring a turkey into range as it is for one. Two hunters create more than twice the noise and motion of one hunter, in part because of the constant temptation, and the occasional need, for the two hunters to communicate with words or gestures. With a good blind, two turkey hunters can hunt together almost as effectively as one.

Bowhunters who prefer to shoot standing, or hunters who have to stand up to relieve back or knee problems, can use taller blinds.

For hunters who are unable for any reason to sit comfortably against a tree, blinds are a godsend. Sometimes the difficulty stems from a back injury, bad knees, or some similar ailment. Sometimes it's just a matter of having a busy disposition. Deer hunters who frequently still-hunt because they don't enjoy remaining in a stand for long periods, for example, will probably not enjoy sitting motionless in the spring turkey woods, either. Still-hunting turkeys is not generally an option. And though some might take issue with this, I believe there are hunters who can sit still enough to hunt deer effectively, but not turkeys.

Only if I think a good buck may be following it do I let a deer go by without putting the crosshairs or the sight pin on it, sometimes raising my gun or bow repeatedly. Try getting away with that kind of movement around a turkey. And what deer hunter has never had a deer approach him, especially in low light conditions, out of curiosity? If any turkeys ever engaged in that kind of behavior, they were eliminated from the gene pool long before I took up the sport.

I suspect most hunters are aware if sitting motionless for long periods is difficult for them, but not all are. Here is one indication, though: If most of the gobblers you take are birds that come gobbling and strutting all the way in, there is a good chance you're being spotted by turkeys. More birds prefer to sneak in quietly, as opposed to strutting in. And most hunters are able to sit still when they see or hear a gobbler approaching. If a hunter never catches birds sneaking in, chances are turkeys are spotting him before he sees them, and usually it is movement that gives hunters away. In any case, blinds are a cure for the problem.

If you enjoy photographing turkeys, blinds are all but essential. It might be possible to get decent photos without a blind, but only the blind enables the photographer to zoom the lens in and out at will, change lenses, change film, turn the camera from horizontal to vertical, or move the camera to photograph different birds in a flock. Photography aside, blinds provide a great way to observe turkeys at length and up close. For the inexperienced hunter, there really is no substitute for observing turkeys as they feed, fight, dust, breed, and go about their normal behavior, not to mention the education gained from listening to the sometimes constant stream of purring, whining, clucking, and yelping that goes on among turkeys.

Author arrowed turkey after photographing it in strut zone. Note blind in background.

Opportunities for this kind of observation of wild turkeys are unusual and fleeting outside the confines of a blind, but common and often long-lasting from inside a good blind. I mentioned earlier that there are situations in which every turkey hunter could make use of a good blind. The first that comes to mind is when hunting wide-open country, like that found in much of the West. I've sat glassing Merriam's for hours at a time from distances of several hundred yards and more, unable to approach them, or move at all, without being seen. Run and gun tactics are simply difficult to employ in that kind of country. It's not that you can't find a good setup and call the birds in. The problem is that you can't move after sunup and before sundown without being spotted. Move around much in that kind of environment and it won't be long before the birds become aware that they are being hunted, making them less vocal, more call shy, and generally even more wary than usual.

Blinds are a good way to hunt turkeys with minimum impact, especially when you're in a relatively small piece of property. Turkeys will quickly become call shy and generally hard to hunt if they're chased around a property by two or three hunters on a regular basis. On the other hand, if the hunters slip quietly into well-placed blinds before first light, and are careful to sneak out without being seen, the same property can be hunted regularly by several hunters, for the length of the season, with little affect on the turkeys' behavior.

Safety is a factor here, as well. Several hunters can hunt the same parcel of real estate quite safely if each is sitting in a blind at some distance from one another. Finally, every turkey hunter eventually confronts a particularly tough-to-kill turkey. The real limb-hangers are four or five years old or more, and chances are most of them get whipped regularly by two- and three-year old birds. Even jakes can often gang up on an old gobbler and run him off. Not surprisingly, these birds become loners, gobbling only a few times on the roost if at all, rarely strutting, and reluctant to approach any hens for fear of a good drubbing. Such gobblers can be almost impossible to call in, and even bushwhacking them is tough. A blind is an ideal way to hunt them.

Types of Blinds

Blinds for turkey hunting come in two categories: 1) natural, or 2) artificial. Either type can be elaborate and sophisticated, or simple. Though at times I've made use of all kinds of blinds, the most effective ones are blinds that consist of a complete, 360-degree enclosure, with a top. Natural blinds consist of rocks, logs, deadfalls, trees, tall grass, and similar debris. It only makes sense, when setting up, to take advantage of naturally occurring cover, and to move a log or prune a few limbs and stick them in the ground for cover, where legal. Hunters who hunt the same place regularly often have several such blinds in different spots in the area, moving from one to another as conditions dictate.

There are disadvantages to these blinds. First, deadfalls, boulders, trees, and other materials aren't always conveniently located. Beyond that, the biggest disadvantage I've found is that if the blind is thick enough to provide good concealment, it also restricts visibility and limits shooting options. Another disadvantage is that few natural blinds provide 360 degrees of concealment. If you're concealed to the front, the right side, and the back, guess where that gobbler's going to sneak in from?

Natural blinds aside, the simplest blinds consist of a piece of camo fabric stretched between two trees. Slightly more versatile models are self-supporting, often consisting of fabric between two poles that are stuck in the ground, while in other cases the blind materials itself is rigid and made of waxed cardboard or ply wood.

Though they can be helpful in hiding the movements required to work a friction call, I have not found these blinds effective enough to warrant carrying them through the woods. Most do not provide 360 degrees of concealment, though some can be made to do so. Those that do usually require hunters to shoot over the top. This defeats the purpose for the bowhunter, but even shotgun hunters must be somewhat exposed in order to shoot over these blinds. It is possible to cut shooting ports in the material, but these openings compromise the effectiveness of the blind in a way that such openings in a fully enclosed blind with a top do not.

Shoot-over binds such as the one pictured can conceal some movement. Hunters are exposed when in position to shoot, though, and may be spotted by birds coming in from an unexpected direction.

The top on a fully enclosed blind darkens the interior. The best blinds are lined in black to increase that effect. The result is that unless the hunter is wearing light colors or puts his uncamouflaged hands or face very close to the opening, a turkey looking into the blind sees only darkness. That effect, together with 360 degrees of concealment around the sides, usually allows hunters to get away with a great deal of movement.

In Chapter 8, I recount an incident in which I sat in an Insta-Coil blind, with several hens around me, and photographed a gobbler as he approached in full strut across a pasture. As the camera rewound after the last frame was exposed, I picked up my bow and put an arrow through the longbeard at twelve yards. No other form of concealment would have allowed me to get away with half that amount of movement.

Blinds such as the Invisi-blind, above, are roomy and comfortable enough for long stays.

Tactics

Modern blinds make it possible for turkey hunters to use the same strategies they might use without blinds, locating gobblers and setting up on them, and relocating as necessary. A less enjoyable (for many hunters) but at least equally effective approach is to put a blind near a likely spot - usually a strut zone - and wait the birds out, calling at regular intervals.

Can blinds spook turkeys? A blind that is flapping in the wind can definitely spook turkeys or any other game. Beyond that, the conventional thinking is that turkeys pay little attention to blinds. I'm not so sure. I think turkeys are sometimes wary around newly erected blinds that are set in the open, and will refuse to come within range of them.

Author believes that turkeys sometimes shy away from newly erected blinds in the open. A little added concealment can make a difference.

Since they don't run or show signs of obvious alarm, and since turkeys are notorious for hanging up anyway, hunters assume they are hanging up for other reasons and are not reacting to the blind. To be on the safe side, I like to put my blinds between or at least next to trees, shrubs, boulders, or other natural cover, and often place logs in front of them or supplement them with a few strategically placed limbs.

Most hunters use decoys when hunting from a blind. Arguments can be made for or against decoys, but properly used, I believe their advantages outweigh their disadvantages. I prefer to use two hens and a jake, but one decoy will sometimes work. When using a jake, keep in mind that a gobbler almost always approaches the jake first, and will circle to get in front of it if necessary. For safety reasons, I put the decoys out at least fifteen yards or so when gun hunting, a little closer when bowhunting.

Given the absence of a tree to lean against, a good seat is essential. A bucket or stool will work, but a chair offers the advantage of back support. I use a fold-up chair without arms, because the arms get in my way when bowhunting.

Selecting a Blind

The perfect blind, like the perfect gun, has not yet been invented. If there were a perfect blind, it would be light and compact for carrying, while being roomy and comfortable in use. The fabric would be waterproof and breathable, quiet and durable. Our perfect blind would go up and down silently in seconds, and would not flap in the wind. It would contain storage pockets, along with loops or hooks on which hunters could hang a bow, gun, or other accessories.

I'm probably leaving out a few desirable qualities, but some of those already mentioned are achievable only at the expense of other desirable qualities. The better blinds introduced in recent years have gone a long way toward minimizing those trade-offs, but at the expense of yet another desirable quality: low cost. The best blinds are not cheap.

When selecting blinds, get your hands on them. A photo and a catalog description won't tell you what you really need to know. Some qualities should not be compromised, and one of them is adequate size. Certainly no hunter wants to sit stooped over for hours at a stretch under a low roof. Bowhunters must have enough room to come to full draw without pushing against the top or back of the blind, or even worrying about it. Even shouldering a shotgun requires more space than you might think. If two people will sometimes be in the blind, it must be big enough to accommodate both.

Does the material seem durable? Is it noisy? Will it be unbearably hot in the sun? Does it go up and down as easily as the manufacturer claims? How much does it weigh? How compactly does it fold up? These are all things to look at. How tight is it when set up? This is important, because loose material flapping in the wind will spook turkeys.

Don't automatically rule out good-quality, older-style blinds that are not so portable or quick to set up. If you have a great spot you can drive to, or walk a very short distance to, or if you are hunting private land in an area where you would feel safe leaving a blind in place for days at a time or for the entire season, these blinds are worth considering. In many cases, they are roomier and more taut than the newer quick-set-up blinds.

If I've given the impression that blinds are guaranteed to fill your tag, that has not been my intention. They can provide the opportunity to observe wild turkeys up close and at length. They can be a real boon to youngsters, to older hunters, or to any hunter who has difficulty sitting on the ground or remaining motionless in one position for long periods. They can make it possible for several hunters to regularly hunt small parcels of land without making turkeys call-shy. And, in the hands of a knowledgeable, experienced turkey hunter, they can help you hunt those elusive long-spurred old gobblers that are nearly impossible to hunt by more conventional means. There are some very good reasons not to use blinds, but hunting effectiveness is not one of them.

New blinds are light and compact enough to go anywhere. Blind above is the popular Insta-Coil.

Tips

• Deer hunters give careful thought not only where they will place tree stands, but how they will access their hunting spots without alerting deer. Turkey hunters should do the same, developing strategies for moving from one strut zone or one part of the woods to another without bumping turkeys. This is especially important for hunting relatively small private properties.

• Handkerchiefs are useful turkey-hunting accessories. When spread over the knees, camo or green/brown hankies can cover the movement of working a friction call. Flap them to imitate flydown or fight sounds. Tie them behind your ears to cover your face if you lose your headnet. Soak them in cool water and put them on your head or around your neck in hot weather. Use fluorescent-orange ones as flags or markers to mark trails, indicate your spot for safety or signal an emergency.

Jonathan Harling of the National Wild Turkey Federation with double bore smokepole, accessories, and a nice Black Hills Merriams.

"Several of our young people were formerly brought up at the Colleges of the Northern Provinces: they were instructed in all your sciences; but, when they came back to us, they were bad Runners, ignorant of every means of living in the woods . . . neither fit for Hunters, Warriors, nor Counselors, they were totally good for nothing."

--Indians of the Six Nations
at Lancaster, Pennsylvania, 1744

Chapter 7

HUNTING WITH MUZZLELOADERS

Finding a good setup in the blackbrush country of South Texas is not often easy, but when a gobbler responded to my aggressive yelps from 100 yards out, I began scrambling for a spot. Nothing to lean against here, a cactus there, too exposed everywhere. The gobbler sounded off again, so close I dropped where I stood and got my gun over my knee.

Then, for ten minutes I heard nothing. Unable to hold the barrel up any longer, and guessing I had spooked the bird, I lowered the gun. When I carefully pulled a crow call from my pocket and screeched out a blast, the turkey thundered back from the other side of a clump of blackbrush not twenty yards away. I clucked, and he clucked back and began purring steadily. Then I heard drumming.

For several minutes I again sat in the open with gun at the ready and heart pounding. When the drumming stopped, I pulled the hammer back on my double-bore muzzleloading shotgun. Right on cue the big Rio Grande walked into the open and stepped onto a log, his red-white-and-blue head vivid against the drab tans and browns of the near-desert habitat. He hopped off the log and, as I lined the beads up on his neck, I was suddenly aware of a second brilliantly hued gobbler coming into view on his right. Already committed, I pulled the trigger; the big 10 gauge bucked and the gray smoke rolled, but the image that ensued did not match the one that had already begun playing in my head--the one in which I almost casually stand and hurry over to collect my prize.

What happened instead was that the gobbler ran off, bird number two right behind him. He did not go down and get back up, nor did he leave any feathers behind. In fact, the big gobbler hadn't even flinched. I'm never quick to assume a clean miss, but this had every appearance of one. I mentally replayed the entire scene over and over. The bird was standing, neck stretched, at about twenty yards. I had literally shot turkeys' heads off at close range with that smokepole, and I was confident my cheek was on the stock and the bead was on his neck.

The explanation hit me as soon as I thought back to my predawn preparations. When I had loaded in the darkness, the over-shot wad I pushed down the right barrel hadn't felt right. I had the sensation that it started crooked and then crumpled in the bore. To be safe--or so I thought--I had pushed a second over-shot card down behind it and tamped it over the first. Clearly that had not worked. I was convinced, and remain convinced, that as soon as I finished loading the second barrel and pointed the gun toward the ground, all the shot rolled out of that right barrel. I hadn't seen it in the dark, and the noise of the guide's truck as he bumped off down the access road prevented my hearing it. The gobbler probably experienced nothing more than a roar and a blast of hot air as the wad zinged by his head!

For the previous five years I had used that smokepole for most of my turkey hunting, and had taken numerous birds with it from Florida to Ohio and several states in between, with never a mishap. I was about to experience a second mishap, right on the heels of the first.

It's difficult to regroup after an experience like that. I walked to a shallow, rocky draw where a few scraggly hackberry trees offered shade, and stood mentally kicking myself for not unloading and reloading when I sensed that the over-shot wad had not gone smoothly down the bore. I tried to concentrate on forming a new strategy for the rest of the morning's hunt. Perhaps ten minutes later--I wasn't even finished beating myself up yet--I heard a cluck and froze. Turning very slowly to peer behind me, I made out the dim shape of a turkey, then another. The two hens moved past me through the thin hackberries and mesquites, followed by a dozen others, all clucking, yelping, and purring continuously as they made their way to a dirt road winding off to my right.

Their noisy clucks and yelps got the attention of another group that was coming over a slight rise down the road to the left. When those birds began yelping, they were cut off by a gobble. I looked down the road and saw the top of a fanned-out turkey tail behind them. I slid down the tree to the ground and got in position, not believing I was back in the game barely ten minutes after pulling the trigger. The hens hurried by, and the gobbler came strutting and drumming up the road at a leisurely pace. Determined not to blow my undeserved second chance, I waited as the big Rio Grande strutted past two small openings through the shrubs to my left, convinced he would follow the same path taken by the hens.

He did exactly that, and when the moment was right, I clucked, he went into a half strut, and I dropped the hammer on barrel two. And had the pop-kaboom! kind of hangfire that undoubtedly disheartened our muzzleloader-toting ancestors on occasion. I felt myself pull off even as the powder ignited, and though feathers floated on the breeze, the big bird had lifted straight up out of the smoke and flown off rapidly at what would have been treetop level, had there been any real trees in the area. Suddenly, at what looked to be about sixty yards, he pitched down and hit the ground with an audible whump. Certain I'd find him dead given the impact, I hurried to the spot I marked and hung an orange trail marker on a bush. I was a very relieved turkey hunter when, more than an hour later, I found the gobbler dead where he had hit the ground--more than fifty yards from my trail marker and 110 paced-off yards from where I had shot him.

Satisfied with my Rio Grande gobbler but not entirely happy with the way things had gone, I sat in the rapidly shrinking shadow of a mesquite bush to ponder the morning's events. I'd already figured out that first misfire, but what had caused the hangfire?

I use Pyrodex regularly in my in-line muzzleloading rifles, but had determined long ago that my scattergun, with sidehammers, prefers black powder. I couldn't board a plane with black powder, though, so before heading for Texas I had phoned a sporting-goods store between the airport and my hunting destination, and was assured that they did indeed carry black powder.

When I arrived, I discovered that they didn't. They carried Pyrodex, not black powder. Rather than drag my hunting partners all over town and delay our arrival in camp, I left with the Pyrodex and some misgivings. All of which is to say this: the blackpowder hunter can, through a little knowledge, practice, and experience, pull the trigger of his firearm confident it will make a clean kill. After five seasons without a misfire or hangfire (when there is a delay between the pulling of the trigger and the igniting of the powder, I was confident both times I pulled the trigger on those Rio Grandes. In fact), I was a little overconfident, and that was the problem. Even in the case of the hangfire, the kind of good follow-through that becomes second nature to every experienced blackpowder hunter would have resulted in a clean kill. A few years of no hangfires with that gun had let me become careless about following through the shot.

It is part of the challenge of hunting with muzzleloaders. The fact is, the hunter who becomes overconfident, gets lazy about cleaning his gun, gets distracted while loading or careless about attending to details (such as not bothering to unload and reload when he feels an over-shot wad going down wrong, or settling for one powder when experience has shown another to be better medicine for his gun), will sooner or later muff a hard-earned opportunity at game. That added challenge, along with the sense of tradition muzzleloaders can imbue in the hunt, is the reason more and more hunters are turning to muzzleloaders. There is something about muzzleloaders and the bird that graced the table on the first Thanksgiving that goes together like--well, like turkey and Thanksgiving.

The Muzzleloading Shotgun

Because a lot of turkey hunters are also deer hunters who take advantage of the special primitive weapons deer hunts offered in most states, many turkey hunters have experience with blackpowder rifles. The muzzleloading rifle gives away a lot to its modern centerfire counterpart. Although rivaling (and in some cases surpassing) the centerfire rifles in terms of accuracy, soot-burning rifles simply cannot match them in terms of range and energy.

That is not a criticism--I regularly hunt with charcoal burners myself, even when I have the option of hunting with a centerfire rifle. But target shooting and advertising hype to the contrary, smokepoles are not suitable for long-range hunting.

Author with smokepole and an Alabama gobbler taken at Bent Creek Lodge in Jachin, Alabama.

The scattergun is different. The smokepole scattergunner may not be able to work up a load that will outperform the latest and best shotshells, but he can come close. Many smokepoles have not been as effective for turkey hunting for two reasons: 1) Most smokepoles have traditionally featured true cylinder bores, which is to say they were unchoked, and those that were choked tended to be choked only moderately; and 2) many hunters did not try to develop loads effective at longer ranges.

Understand that not every hunter demands that his smokepole match modern shotguns in range. Many hunters prefer a traditional gun modeled after old fowling pieces, and welcome the challenge imposed by the more limited range. For the same reason, they are not interested in developing special loads designed solely to extend range. They know the maximum effective range of their gun and the load they are using, and they hunt accordingly. And, of course, if their gun does double duty for hunting grouse, woodcock, or upland birds, the open choke is a desirable feature, not a handicap.

The questions are, how much of a challenge do you seek, and just how traditional do you wish to be? For practical hunting purposes, at one end of the scale we can put a flintlock cylinder- bore scattergun; at the other end of the scale would be a modern, in-line smokepole featuring an extra-full turkey choke tube and any extras that might be found on a modern shotgun, including camo patterns, fiber-optic sights or a scope, and a sling. While various ignition systems and other factors might make one scattergun more challenging to use than another, the potential effective range is determined largely by choke. It would be possible, for instance, to have a flintlock jug-choked, or threaded for choke tubes (assuming the barrel is thick enough), in which case its range could approach that of most modern shotguns. Jug-choking entails opening up the bore behind the muzzle, so that the pattern expands for an interval before being constricted again into the original bore size before exiting the muzzle.

A competent gunsmith can perform either of these alterations at a reasonable cost. My own arsenal includes a 12-gauge Traditions in-line muzzleloader that is relatively short and light (43 1/2" total length and about 7 1/2 pounds), with a durable, good-looking black synthetic stock and a matte-black barrel, a sling, and a light-gathering sight pin. Veteran blackpowder writer and industry consultant Hank Strong worked up a load for that smokepole that enables it to outperform most of my modern shotguns. I hesitate to state maximum ranges, because there are naturally differences of opinion about how many shot must hit on or close to a turkey's spine to be consistently lethal, not to mention the whole issue of downrange energy, but I can say confidently, and using the most conservative judgment, that that gun with the right load will kill turkeys at forty yards every time. I wouldn't argue with any observer who claimed forty-five yards or more. Also in my collection is a Cabela's 10-gauge double bore made by Italian gunmaker David Pedersoli.

It is threaded for choke tubes, but the double barrels prevent using the kind of extended extra-full tubes that make for the tightest patterns. I've had fun for years trying to work up a load that will get me a forty-yard maximum range out of that gun--and I'm not done trying--but so far the best I can do is thirty-five yards. Nonetheless, it's one of my favorite turkey guns. It's a handsome gun, with the look and feel of a traditional caplock fowling piece, while chromed barrels (for steel shot) and choke tubes give me the options of hunting waterfowl, pheasants, and other game. For me, that gun is an ideal blend of traditional styling with a few modern touches that increase its range and versatility.

Author's 10 gauge double-bore Pedersoli from Cabela's, with a long-bearded Osceola.

Developing A Load

Patterning any shotgun that will be used for turkey hunting is important; for the frontstuffer, it is doubly so. A given muzzleloader may be effective at twenty yards or at forty yards or more, depending upon the load. In effect, every shot from a muzzleloader is a hand load.

Patterning any shotgun is important for turkey hunting; it's even more important in the case of muzzleloaders.

Powder

The first component of any load is the powder. If you are new to muzzle-loading, one point cannot be emphasized enough: Never, ever shoot any kind of modern smokeless powder through a muzzleloader. Black powder is the original, traditional powder for muzzleloaders, but there are blackpowder substitutes on the market. Let's look at black powder first.

Black powder is available in varying granulations. The coarsest granulations are suitable for use in cannons, while the finer granulations are used for small-bore pistols and for pan powder in flintlocks. For our purposes, only Fg, a fairly course granulation, through granulations up to FFFg, are of any real concern. Far and away the most popular granulation of black powder is FFg, which works well in 45-caliber and bigger rifles, as well as in all the popular shotgun bores. Fg, though less popular, works well in 12 bores and even better in 10 bores. It is important to understand that finer granulations develop higher bore pressures. I would not recommend experimenting with granulations finer than those recommended by a gun's manufacturer. Black powder is generally loaded by volume. In 12 bores, seventy to 100 grains of black powder would fall in the range of the most commonly used loads.

Black powder is listed as a Class A explosive. Storing small volumes of it is reasonably safe if you treat it as you would any highly flammable material, such as gasoline. It keeps well if kept in cool, dark places, but can degrade over time. Black powder remains popular as a muzzleloading propellant not only because it is the only choice for those interested in historical authenticity, but because it offers at least one advantage over the alternatives. That advantage is indicated by its Class A rating-meaning that black powder ignites at a lower temperature than black powder substitutes do. In the simplest terms, it's easier to set off. In some firearms, especially the modern in-line guns, this is not often a factor.

Many hunters, myself included, believe that the difference can be very noticeable in flintlocks or percussion guns with traditional locks, particularly those using sidehammers. (In effect, the spark on some sidehammer guns must travel around a corner to reach the powder in the breech.) Why use blackpowder substitutes? They offer some advantages. Various blackpowder substitutes have come and gone over the years, but few have stood the test of time, and hunters have learned to be skeptical of them. The major exception is Pyrodex. Pyrodex offers several advantages over black powder.

First, because it is listed as a Class B explosive, it is easier to obtain. Black powder must be shipped and stored according to stringent regulations. Many sporting-goods stores offer Pyrodex right off the shelf. Pyrodex is cleaner burning than black powder, meaning that cleaning up is easier. Black powder leaves a lot of solid residue in the barrel. It's possible to reload a time or two without cleaning up, but loading gets progressively more difficult and soon becomes impossible. With Pyrodex, that problem is greatly reduced.

Larry Norton of Alabama's Bent Creek Lodge with smokepole and longbeard.

Some argue that Pyrodex, while being cleaner-burning than black powder, is more corrosive. Others argue that it is less so. I know of no independent scientific evidence to confirm either view. Both Pyrodex and black powder are hygroscopic, which is to say they attract and hold moisture. Post-shooting clean-up is essential, and a failure to do so will sooner or later result in a ruined barrel.

Pyrodex is loaded volume for volume with black powder. Given the relative inefficiency of black powder and Pyrodex -- a difference of five grains by volume makes no measurable difference in velocity -- I cannot imagine why anyone measures loads by weight. It's important to understand, though, that while black powder and Pyrodex may be used interchangeably by volume, they are not interchangeable by weight.

Pyrodex is granulated much as black powder is. It is also available in various grades, including Pyrodex Select. Select is alleged to produce more consistent velocities, and some match rifle shooters prefer it. I doubt that it could make a noticeable difference for the shotgunner.

Two other blackpowder substitutes on the market are Clean Shot, from Clean Shot Technologies, Inc., in Whitewater, Colorado, and Clear Shot, by long-time blackpowder maker Goex of Doyline, Louisiana. As Class B explosives both powders should, like Pyrodex, be easier to obtain. Both powders claim, as did other blackpowder substitutes before them, to avoid the smell, corrosiveness, and clean-up chores associated with black powder. I have tested Clean Shot and had excellent results with it. After a year of storage, it appears to be in good condition. (Rapid deterioration in storage has been among the problems of other BP substitutes.) My tests haven't been extensive enough to rule out any problems, but several serious shooters I know have been using it extensively for more than a year and swear by it. Goex's Clear Shot has similarly received rave reviews from some serious and knowledgeable shooters testing pre-production samples. It is making its appearance on the market as I write, and I have not had the opportunity to test it.

Smokepole and blue-grass gobbler taken on a Kentucky hunt.

Wads

Wads have a major effect on shot patterns. Simply varying the type of wad used, or the thickness of the wad, will alter the pattern. Most BP scattergunners use an over-powder wad designed primarily to create a gas seal and prevent the expanding gases from blowing around the wad, thereby reducing volume and probably ruining the pattern. This is followed by a thicker felt wad, designed to cushion the shot from impact. This improves the pattern and reduces the number of 'flyers' created when round shot are deformed. After this comes the shot charge itself -- more about that later--followed by a thin, over-shot wad designed primarily to prevent the shot from rolling out the barrel when the gun is pointed down. The over-shot wads can and often do affect patterns; shooters sometimes alter patterns by using thinner or lighter cards, or by using two cards together. Hank Strong insists he has improved his patterns by using homemade over-shot cards that he cuts from plastic foam.

The plastic shot cups that have tightened the patterns of modern shotshells can do the same for the muzzleloader. (If you have a barrel suitable for use with steel shot and intend to use steel shot, a plastic cup designed for that purpose is essential.) Some experimentation is usually required, and many hunters alter shot cups by trimming them, splitting them if they're not split, or even taping them if they are. There is no guarantee these will produce better patterns. I've tried several varieties of shot cups in my beloved Cabela's Pedersoli, with no detectable difference in the pattern. I have seen cases in which the tightest patterns were produced by using a plastic shot cup with a modified-choke tube. One thing important to note about plastic shot cups is that they produce plastic fouling in the bore. This is less of a problem than that caused by plastic sabots in rifles, but in both cases the plastic fouling must occasionally be removed. Many good gun-cleaning solvents will take care of the problem. The traditional hot water and soap cleaning method will not.

It is extremely important that wads fit properly. Obtaining proper fit is somewhat complicated by the fact that, with muzzleloaders, gauges are not always exactly as stated. A nominal 12 gauge may in reality be closer to a 13 gauge, a 10 gauge may really be an 11 gauge, and so on. This makes it easy to use shotshell components in muzzleloaders, since they must be sized smaller to fit inside the shotshell. That is, the smaller components designed to fit inside a 12-gauge shotshell will fit nicely inside a 13-gauge muzzleloader. If the stated gauge is the actual gauge, though, these components would be too small. This could (and probably would) affect performance. Wads that are too big, on the other hand, will be very difficult to load, and may create a safety hazard. At some point a wad (or any other component of the load) may cease to be a projectile, and become an obstruction in the bore. While I would never recommend a powder charge beyond the conservative powder charges recommended by the manufacturer, it is a bore obstruction that creates the biggest hazard for the smokepole shooter, even when the powder charge is modest.

Proper fit aside, anything in the bore becomes an obstruction and a hazard if it is not seated firmly against the powder charge. Hunters needn't lean on their ramrods, or apply a great deal of pressure, but it is important to know that the entire charge is all the way down the bore. The best way to do this is to mark the ramrod after the proper load has been developed. Cut a notch in it or, or draw a line on it, even with the muzzle. If the ramrod stops short of that line, the charge isn't fully seated, or the gun has been double-charged.

Russ Markesbery of Markesbery Muzzleloaders with a fine Kentucky bluegrass gobbler.

One of the reasons early scatterguns weren't choked is that chokes make loading more difficult. This is especially true of modern extra-full turkey choke tubes. You might, through experimentation, find a good wad that will fit through a tight choke and still provide a good seal. Thompson/Center makes a wad called the Natural Wad that works nicely for many hunters, as does Ox-Yoke's Wonder Wad. Both are prelubed and designed to deform going through the choke, then expand to fill the barrel again.

Another option, in the case of guns with choke tubes, is to pour in the powder, remove the tubes, push the wads down the bore, followed by the shot and the over-shot card, then replace the tubes. (It's necessary to put the powder down the bore before removing the tubes, so powder won't get in the delicate threads.) This might sound like a hassle, but the turkey hunter hopes to get one shot. Frequent reloading is not something the turkey hunter normally does. If the same gun is used for waterfowl or upland game, chances are that more open choke tubes will be used, and removing these should not be necessary.

The Shot Charge

In some respects, selecting the right shot for a muzzleloader is similar to selecting the right shot for a shotshell. Smaller sizes often (but not always) produce

Muzzleloading is a paraphernalia-intensive undertaking, which is part of the fun -- a part of the curse, depending on your perspective.

denser patterns, but at a loss of energy downrange. Adding shot up to the maximum recommended weight may improve patterns, but again it is not unusual for a smaller shot charge to pattern better than a larger one, and experimenting with these variables is the only way to find out. Traditionalists like to use the same volume of powder and shot. That works fine for quail hunting, not so well for turkey hunting. I usually get the best results by using the maximum amount of shot, slightly less than the maximum amount of powder. Copper- or nickel-plated shot is hard to find, but will almost always produce better patterns. Short of that, the harder the shot the better. One reliable source I've found for copper- and nickel-plated shot is Ballistic Products, Inc. of Hamel, Minnesota (612/494-9237).

Care And Feeding
of the Muzzleloading Scattergun

The key to reliable ignition in a muzzleloader can be expressed in two words: 'clean' and 'dry'. If the gun is completely clean and completely dry, pulling the trigger will, by any of several various methods depending on the lock type, ignite the powder in the breech and Voila! The gun goes boom. If it does not, odds are ten to one that a lack of cleanliness prevented the spark from reaching the powder, or moisture in the powder prevented it from igniting. Water is the most obvious source of moisture, but probably not the most common cause of misfires or hang-fires today. That honor goes to oil. Generations of hunters have been taught that a properly cared for gun is a well-oiled gun. It's no surprise, then, that when a hunter gets his first muzzleloader, he oils it up after cleaning it. Modern, highly penetrating oils do what they are made to do, and seep into every tiny fissure they contact. They do the reverse, too--they seep out of every tiny fissure. When that happens in the case of muzzleloaders, they seep into the powder, which readily absorbs them. The result is a hangfire--a delay in firing--or a misfire, which is a complete failure to discharge.

Avoid the problem by using very small amounts of oil. When I use oil in the bore, I often apply it in the form of prelubed patches, which tend to coat the barrel with a fine sheen. Another option is to use one of the solid lubes such as Wonder-Lube, or Ox-Yoke, which are less likely to soak into the powder and which tend to make clean up easier. On nipple threads and choke tube threads I like to use small amounts of grease, which is more apt to stay where I want it and less apt to go where I don't than is oil. Automotive anti-seize grease works very well for this, by the way. Before loading the gun, always run a dry, clean cloth down the barrel at least twice. Then, in the case of a percussion gun, fire one or two caps through it. By putting a patch over the end of the barrel, or holding the end of the barrel over a leaf or similar object, it is easy to determine that the nipple vent and barrel are unobstructed, because the patch will blow off the muzzle, or the leaf will move when the blast from the cap reaches it. Then look to make sure no fragments of the cap are left in the face of the hammer, or over the nipple. Run a nipple pick through the nipple vent, and you are ready to load.

I used to occasionally skip firing a cap because making noise near my hunting area went against my instincts. Now, if performing this ritual somewhere shortly before I arrive in my hunting area is not feasible, I do it where I'll be hunting. Believe me, if you fail to perform this simple standard procedure religiously, you will sooner or later regret it. On a related subject, it's a good idea to replace nipples every season or two, depending on how much shooting you do. They cost only a few dollars, and though they may last much longer than one or two seasons, you don't want to find out the hard way that they need replacing.

The traditional method of cleaning the muzzleloader involves the use of hot, soapy water. It works well, so long as the water is very hot and there is no copper or plastic fouling in the barrel. If your gun is equipped with choke tubes, remove them and clean them separately, or the threads will rust. You'll naturally avoid getting water into the lock mechanism, which is most easily achieved by removing the barrel before cleaning.

I have no argument with those who, in the interest of maintaining historical authenticity, prefer to use the soap-and-hot-water cleaning method. For my own part, I do my best to keep water as far away from my firearms as possible, and that includes my muzzleloaders. A frontiersman might have had few other options. I have plenty of options, including some outstanding solvents that will remove all the powder fouling as well as any copper or plastic residues, and with much less risk of rusting any parts of my gun. Remington makes a good solvent, as does Shooter's Choice and several other companies. Black Off, by Rusty Duck Premium Gun Care Products, offers the advantage of not only removing whatever materials I can manage to foul my barrel with, but of evaporating very fast. That's convenient on the range, when I'm cleaning between shots and don't want to spend a lot of time swabbing moisture out of the bore. It also leaves me a little less concerned that cleaning my gun will rust it. We've already indicated the importance of keeping nipples clean. The best and easiest way to clean them is to soak them in solvent while you clean the barrels.

Occasionally, it's necessary to remove the lock mechanism and clean it. I remove mine about twice a year. I often look at it and put it back without touching it, being a firm believer in the 'if it ain't broke don't fix it' school of gunsmithing. Adjusting lock mechanisms or trigger pulls can be very tricky with muzzleloaders, and is probably best left to a gunsmith. Trigger pulls on muzzleloading shotguns tend to be very heavy, though, and in some cases a little lubrication will lighten them significantly.

Finally, wood stocks need attention from time to time. I take my guns apart when they're new and put several coats of boiled linseed oil on all the wood, then rub it down periodically with new applications. One of the great things about muzzleloaders is that they are comparatively simple devices. They don't call them sootburners for nothing: Black powder is dirty, and the clean-up requires a little more time and effort than is the case for modern firearms. But if you keep them clean and dry, they will shoot reliably year after year.

Hunting With the Muzzleloading Shotgun

Aside from the probable limited range and the one-shot capability (except with double bores), hunting with a muzzleloader differs in only a few ways from hunting with a pump gun or autoloader. First, there is more paraphernalia associated with muzzleloaders. Some hunters consider this part of the charm of muzzleloaders; others find it a source of frustration. Losing or forgetting one small item, such as a nipple wrench, can ruin a hunt. Many hunters carry a possibles bag with all the necessary paraphernalia. All the items can easily fit inside a hunting vest, but the bag has the advantage of being one item to pack or remember, as opposed to numerous small items.

Turkey hunting is normally a one-shot game, but the day you go afield without extra ammunition is the day you'll need a second shot--unless you're hunting with a double bore, in which case you'll need a third shot. Trust me on this, I've been there. Plastic film canisters make convenient speed loaders. Put premeasured powder loads in a couple of canisters, wads and premeasured shot charges in a couple of others.Hunting in the rain is a challenge for the muzzleloader. Modern, lubricated wads form a seal that normally prevents water from reaching the powder through the barrel, but some hunters put a balloon over the muzzle anyway. This works, and doesn't seem to affect patterns. A piece of electrical tape works, too.

A more likely conduit for water reaching the powder is through the nipple or the flash pan. Oiled leather boots that fit over the locks are the traditional preventatives, and these are available, along with other muzzleloading supplies, from the companies listed at the end of this chapter. In a pinch, a plastic sandwich bag will do the job. Hunting in the rain is an added challenge, but our muzzleloader-toting ancestors did it routinely. Rain aside, moisture can reach the powder through simple condensation. In hunting, camps, hunters often leave their guns loaded overnight, sometimes for days at a time. This is fine as long as they are uncapped before being brought into tents or cabins. The problem is that the barrels are brought into the warmth from out in the cold, and condensation forms moisture in the barrel. It's better to leave guns locked in a vehicle overnight, or on a porch, alcove, or other area where the guns will not be subjected to rapid temperature changes.

Deer hunters have the excuse of special, primitive-weapons deer seasons for owning and using muzzleloaders. There are no such primitive weapons turkey seasons that I'm aware of, so we muzzleloading turkey hunters have no excuse. Fortunately, no excuse is required. We do it because it's fun, or we do it because it is a tad more challenging, or we do it because walking out of the woods with a turkey slung over one shoulder and a muzzleloader in hand offers us a unique glimpse into our nation's past. Every serious turkey hunter owes it to himself to sooner or later give muzzleloading a try.

Sources of Blackpowder Supplies and Accessories

Mountain State Muzzleloading, Inc.
#1 Muzzleloading Place
Williamstown, WV 26187
304/375-7842; FAX 304/375-3737
www.mtnstatemuzzleloading.com

Dixie Gunworks
Hwy. 51 South
Union City, TN 38261
order 800/238-6785; FAX 901/885-0440
www.dixiegun.com

Ox-Yoke Originals, Inc.
34 W. Main St.
Milo, ME 04463
207/943-7351; FAX 207/943-2416
www.oxyoke.com

Thompson/Center Arms
P.O. Box 5002
Rochester, NH 03866
603/332-2394; FAX 603/332-5133
www.tcarms.com

Cabela's
One Cabela Dr.
Sidney, NE 69160
order 800/237-4444; FAX 800/496-6329
www.cabelas.com

Rusty Duck Premium Gun Care Products
7785 Foundation Dr. Ste. 6
Florence, KY 41042
859/342-5553; FAX 859/342-2380
www.rustyduck.com

Muzzleloader Safety Tips

The same basic safety rules that apply to all firearms apply equally to muzzleloaders, with a few additional issues to keep in mind, including the following:

Never pour powder directly from a container or flask into the barrel. On the range, keep powder containers closed.

Wait a minute, or swab the bore carefully, before reloading a fired barrel, to make sure no smoldering powder lingers in the barrel.

When the gun fails to discharge, point the barrel in a safe direction and wait two minutes before attempting to fire it again or unload it.

When reloading one barrel of a double bore, be sure to first remove the cap from the other barrel.

To avoid double charges and similar loading mishaps, mark a reference point on your ramrod, even with the end of the muzzle. This will tell you if the right load is properly seated.

Be especially careful when loading double bore guns. Use your ramrod to check and make sure you haven't put two charges in one barrel.

Wear shooting glasses to protect against blowback or percussion cap fragments.

Firing a round through one barrel of a double bore can cause the load in the other barrel to partially dislodge and move down bore, creating a hazard. Uncap the second barrel, or remove the powder from the firing pan, and use the ramrod to ensure that the second load is properly seated after firing the first.

A New/Old Trick For Tightening Patterns in Muzzleloading Shotguns

One of the more important developments contributing to the effectiveness of modern shotshells is the use of plastic buffers. I was sure I wasn't the only blackpowder shotgunner who had ever attempted to used buffered shot in his frontstuffer only to find that the heavier shot drops instantly to the breech while the buffer floats gently down the bore to end up on top of the shot, where it accomplishes nothing. Then I came across an article by Black Powder Hunting columnist Ross Seyfried, which not only confirmed I wasn't alone in my futile attempts, but which went on to solve the problem.

Seyfried knew from research that English shotgunners as far back as the flintlock era regularly made use of highly sophisticated paper and even wire mesh "cartridges." Various designs were developed to produce different pattern densities, depending on the species hunted and the expected range. One variation included the use of bone dust as a buffering agent.

Seyfried succeeded in developing a modern counterpart to the bone-dust buffered cartridge. I tried it and found, as did Seyfried, that it can significantly tighten patterns and increase range, especially in unchoked, or moderately choked, guns. Here is how it works.

You'll need a dowel, or a cylinder of some sort, and fairly heavy paper, such as twenty-four-pound typing paper. Tight-fitting cartridges don't work well, so you'll want to make slightly under-sized paper tubes. (This is not a problem so long as your over-powder wads fit well.) Wrap the paper around the dowel until you have two complete wraps, then glue the seam. Pull the paper tube up just past the end of the dowel, crimp it, and glue it. Next, cut the paper to form a paper "cartridge" with one end open. The length of each cartridge will depend on the size of your shot charge, so you'll have to experiment a little. You'll want it long enough to contain all the shot, with enough paper left over to crimp or twist closed at the top.

Fill each cartridge with shot and plastic buffer (or bone dust, if you're a strict traditionalist), and crimp or twist the top closed. Shake the cartridge gently as necessary while filling it to ensure even distribution of the buffer. To load, pour powder down the breech and seat the over-powder wad as you normally would. Open the top of the cartridge and drop it down the bore. (This is important. If the cartridge is closed, you may end up with a bullet instead of a shot pattern. Trim off excess paper if necessary.) Carefully seat your over-shot wad, prime the pan or cap the nipple, and you're loaded for bear-or turkey, anyway.

Trophy Scoring

Scoring a wild turkey is not that difficult. Here is the National Wild Turkey Federation formula:

Score=body weight + beard length (X2) + right spur (x10) + left spur (X10)

The body weight is in pounds and other measurements are in inches, but all are converted to decimals for final scoring. (Each 1/16 pound equals .0625 lbs., each 1/8 inch equals .1250 inches.)

The beard is properly measured from the base to the end of the longest filament. Straighten the beard carefully: usually there are one or two filaments that are longer than the others. Each filament is delicate, and the score will be adversely affected if that filament is lost.

Spurs should be measured along the outside of the curve. A tape is one way to do it, but if a ruler is the only measure available, a length of string can be used. Mark the string carefully, and then measure the markings on the string. Bending a stiff piece of paper or a card over the outside of the spur works well, too.

Let's look at a hypothetical turkey of 21 1/2 lbs. with a beard of 10 7/8", a right spur of 1 1/4" and a left spur of 1 3/8".

Converting the turkey's weight is simple enough and gives us a decimal figure of 21.5. The beard in decimals is 10.88. The right spur is 1.25 and the left is 1.38. Then we double the beard and multiply the spurs by 10.

Weight: 21.5
Beard X 2: 21.76
RS X 10: 12.50
LS X 10: 13.80

Total score: 69.56

"There is a passion for hunting something deeply implanted in the human breast."

--Charles Dickens, Oliver Twist, 1838

Chapter 8

BOWHUNTING TURKEYS

Bowhunting turkeys is widely regarded as one of hunting's most challenging endeavors. I certainly would not have argued with that assessment seven or eight seasons ago, when I chased turkeys with a bow in four states unsuccessfully. I wouldn't have taken exception to it five or six seasons ago, when I sat cramped in a blind near an Alabama chufa patch all day for four days with similar results. Most recently, I wouldn't have disagreed with it when I spent three days sweating in a blind in south Texas only to miss what should have been an easy shot at a long-legged Rio Grande gobbler standing in the open not fifteen paces away. I was so stiff after not moving in that blind for three days that when the big moment came, I had to strain for all I was worth to get to full draw. My hands were shaking and my bow felt like some strange new contraption instead of the familiar, fast, quiet, smooth-drawing weapon it had proved itself to be on deer and wild boar. The arrow missed by half a foot, and I sat in silent defeat in the pick-up truck on the long, bumpy ride back to the bunkhouse.

There is a line between "challenging" and "almost impossible," and many hunters consider bowhunting turkeys to be too close to the "almost impossible" side of the ledger. For the bowhunter who is persistent, though, there will come a day when everything falls into place. If he keeps at it, those days will begin to happen more often. On a recent hunt in Ohio, I watched a boss gobbler approach from 200 yards away in a pasture. I was in an Insta-Coil blind, but with three hens pecking all around me, two of them almost close enough to reach out and grab, I remained frozen. The gobbler was in full strut, and never came out of it except to stop and breed a hen about eighty yards out. I was photographing the gobbler all the way in.

At twenty yards I hit the last frame on a roll of film, and the camera began rewinding. It always surprises me when turkeys don't react to that sound, but the fact is that they rarely do. I reached down slowly, picked up my bow, drew, and released when the gobbler was twelve yards away. The big open-on-impact broadhead spined him, and he dropped like a bag of wet sand.

Dedicated hunters such as LeRoy Braungardt, of Missouri, and Iowa bowhunter Roger Raisch were among those who showed the way for modern bow-toting turkey hunters, and I'm far from the only bowhunter who learned a great deal from them.

Oh, what a feeling! Hunters who take a turkey with a bow have joined an elite fraternity.

These days there are hunters who fill their turkey tag with a bow every season. Some fill multiple tags with a bow every season. Clearly, it can be done. And though it remains a challenging undertaking, several comparatively recent developments have made the challenge less daunting.

The New Blinds

The first and perhaps most important of these developments has been improvements in blinds. One of the primary challenges of hunting turkeys with a bow is drawing the bow without being spotted. Braungardt and Raisch insisted years ago that the most consistently effective way to take turkeys with a bow was to use a blind religiously. They scouted hard to find spots they were convinced turkeys were using regularly, then set up large, fully enclosed blinds to call and wait the birds out, resisting the temptation to get up and go after any gobblers that seemed to be hung up or intent on going elsewhere.

Many hunters rejected that style of hunting. They objected to lugging big, heavy blinds around. They didn't like spending ten or fifteen minutes setting up the blinds, and taking them down. They felt the lack of mobility imposed by blinds made them less effective turkey hunters, and the discipline required to sit waiting out the birds when they could hear them gobbling in the distance took some of the fun out of the sport. I had mixed feelings about blinds myself. I used them for photographing turkeys and for taking youngsters or fidgety beginners hunting. Eventually, I came to consider them necessary evils for bowhunting turkeys. I shared all the frustrations mentioned above, but found bowhunting without a blind at least equally frustrating.

My hat is off to those bowhunters who insist on hunting without a blind. However, my own experience led me to believe that the turkey hunter who finds himself within bow range of a gobbler has in most cases put in a lot of time, and used up most of his skill and no small amount of luck. To then expect the gobbler to walk behind a large, conveniently located tree or rock, or to turn facing away in full strut and remain in that position, so the hunter can come to full draw without being spotted, is to make luck a bigger factor than I want it to be in that situation. (Of course if more than one bird comes in, the chances of drawing the bow without being spotted are almost zero, even if a gobbler does cooperate by walking behind a tree or turning away in full strut.) I confirmed for myself what Braungardt, Raisch, and others had been saying for years: The bowhunter who hunts without a blind must be prepared to bring in a lot of gobblers before getting a decent shot at one. By contrast, the bowhunter who brings a gobbler into range while concealed in a blind can usually get off a good shot.

Author with southern Ohio gobbler arrowed from blind in background.

77

Apart from the huge advantage of being able to get shots at unalerted gobblers, over the years I couldn't help but notice a few other things that greatly reduced my frustration with blinds. First, I noticed that my lack of mobility did not decrease the number of turkeys I saw or got within range of. In fact, if I was hunting with another hunter, I saw more turkeys from a blind, assuming I was hunting an area I had scouted or was familiar with. While I missed traveling light and being highly mobile, the notion that being free to chase and set up on numerous gobblers all over the woods will result in seeing more turkeys is, over the long run, an illusion. The hunter who is familiar enough with an area to know where the turkeys are going to strut, feed, dust, or rest, or which ridgelines, logging roads, trails, or other routes they are going to use in traveling between these areas, can see as many or more turkeys by setting up in these areas as by chasing gobblers through the woods and setting up on them. They can also do it without disturbing birds and decreasing gobbling activity or changing other patterns. Then, too, I began to appreciate the unique advantages of a blind. If I gave up some freedom and mobility, I gained comfort and relaxation. I could move in a blind, even with a tom in sight; I could scratch where it itched, knock a bug off my face, change positions. I could even stand up and stretch in some blinds. I could drink coffee in a blind. I traded my little folding stool for a bigger folding chair. There are less pleasant ways to spend a spring morning than sitting comfortably in a blind drinking coffee, reading a good book, and pausing now and then to look around, scratch out a few hen yelps, and listen to the woods coming to life.

While enjoying these advantages, I still considered blinds to be a necessary evil - heavy, cumbersome, and limiting the mobility I enjoyed whether it really was more productive or not. Then came the Insta-Coil blind, followed quickly by a number of other fully enclosed blinds that are light, compact when not in use, and which can be set up or taken down in seconds. Now the limitations on mobility are slight, and I can see no reason for a bowhunter not to take advantage of them. Any hunter whose style is cramped by the old-style blinds (which still have some advantages and a definite niche in the hunting world, by the way), can use one of these newer blinds and feel free to chase gobblers and set up on them as he has always done, setting up and taking down the blinds in seconds, relocating at will, yet still enjoying the advantage of being able to draw on a gobbler without being seen.

Selecting a good blind is difficult, partly because there are a number of excellent ones on the market. Most have their advantages and disadvantages. I've limited my discussion to fully enclosed blinds because, for the bowhunter, other types are inadequate in my opinion. I could never see the advantage in the shoot-over style blind, for instance. If a hunter has to rise above the blind to shoot, the advantage of the blind is all but lost. If the blind does not encircle the hunter, a bird is sure to come in from the unexpected direction. A top on a blind is important, too. It keeps the inside of the blind dark, limiting a turkey's ability to see through the shooting ports or peep holes into the blind. Without the top, the movement required to draw the bow will sometimes be spotted by a sharp-eyed gobbler.

The perfect blind has yet to be invented; all involve trade-offs of one sort or another. The lightest ones are apt to move in the wind, which can spook turkeys. The blinds that are less likely to flap in the wind are more likely to be heavy, or may require a little more time to set up. Some blind materials are quieter than others. There is the issue of durability. Cost is always a factor, and as you might expect, the best blinds are usually among the more expensive. Some blinds that are perfect for gun hunting or photography are inadequate for bowhunting. A bowhunting blind must be tall enough to accommodate a drawn bow, depending on whether the bowhunter wishes to stand while shooting, sit on a stool or chair, sit on the ground, or kneel.

The primary difficulty in bowhunting turkeys is drawing the bow without being seen. Blinds eliminate the problem.

The blind must be deep enough to accommodate the bowhunter at full draw. If an elbow pushes against the back of the blind at full draw, the blind is too small. Blinds do not guarantee success, of course, but they do offer advantages, especially for the bowhunter. It can almost feel like cheating to have a gobbler approach the blind in complete confidence as you shift position, sip coffee, change calls, get your bow in position, and draw, without being seen. There are a few caveats about using blinds for turkey hunting. The wind can be a real bugaboo. A blind that flaps in the wind will usually spook birds. Also, it is possible for a gobbler to spot movement inside the blind. They don't often, but they can. Usually this happens when a hunter puts his face right up to the shooting port to look around. Stay back from the openings in the blind, and if it is dark inside and you are wearing camo, or at least dark clothing, you probably won't be spotted. I always wear a headnet or camo face paint, though I don't leave the headnet on all the time. Try to keep your bow or arrow as far back as you can from the openings, keeping in mind you must be certain the arrow will pass cleanly through the openings. Some blinds have dark interiors, or offer black interiors as an option, and these are worthwhile if not essential features.

Do turkeys ever react to the blinds themselves? Conventional wisdom is that turkeys rarely notice blinds, but I don't accept that entirely. I think that a turkey will sometimes notice a blind that is set in the open, and may react negatively to it on first encountering it. Typically the negative reaction is not to spook and run, but to hang up and refuse to come closer. Because they aren't visibly frightened, hunters think they are hanging up for other reasons, and don't attribute it to the blind. To be on the safe side, I'm inclined to set up blinds inside the tree line when hunting a meadow or other opening. If that isn't an option, I try to at least put the blind beside a tree or shrub, and to add a little extra camo in the form of logs, limbs, or leaves.

Broadheads

The vitals of a turkey are relatively small. Turkeys also have the ability to fly or run for some distance after taking a serious, even fatal hit. Few game animals drop in their tracks, but no game animals are as difficult to track as are turkeys. Our normal reaction as bowhunters, when encountering game that is difficult to put down, is to go with bigger broadheads to cause more damage and create better blood trails. For most bowhunters, bigger broadheads are less accurate. A slight loss of precision is acceptable for deer because they present big targets. Turkeys present small targets and, except in rare instances, do not leave a visible blood trail.

The solution is mechanical, or open-on-impact, broadheads. Whatever you may think of them for big-game hunting - and I have some reservations about them - they are ideal for turkey hunting. The good ones do indeed fly like field points, for precise, accurate shooting. They also open to as much as two or two and one-half inches, which punches quite a hole, greatly increasing the chances of hitting the vitals, spining the bird, or breaking a leg, any of which will put the bird down on the spot. (A turkey with a broken leg cannot usually get off the ground to fly.) The chief complaint about mechanical heads is that they impede penetration. Penetration is not an issue with turkeys.

Rangefinding Devices

Laser rangefinders are a boon to turkey hunters, bowhunters in particular. I've tried the old-style split-screen rangefinders and found them slow and not very precise - on the other hand, my vision is not what it used to be. If they work for you, they work. I do recommend the newer laser rangefinders. Readouts are almost instantaneous, and they are accurate to within a yard at bowhunting ranges. I would-n't think of turkey hunting without mine. Get set up and take a few readings on near-by trees, shrubs, or rocks, and you've established a perimeter inside which you can shoot with confidence. See Chapter 11 for a more in-depth discussion of rangefinding devices.

String Trackers

These are hardly new, but many bowhunters won't pursue turkeys without them. Their effect on accuracy is minimal out to reasonable ranges, and they can help recover turkeys. They are frequently criticized as being less than foolproof - a strange criticism considering that no method is foolproof. The string can break. It usually doesn't, but it can, in which case the hunter is no worse off than those not using a string tracker.

Many bowhunters consider string trackers essential equipment when hunting turkeys.

Used properly, a string tracker will lead bowhunters straight to the turkey. Some bowhunters prefer stoppers on arrows, but most experts find them unnecessary.

There are some downsides: They add weight to the bow, for example, and can unbalance it slightly. Hunters who insist on the mobility to bowhunt outside a blind may find that the string gets caught on weeds or limbs. Still, the disadvantages are minor, and hunters looking to take a turkey with a bow owe it to themselves and their quarry to try these devices.

The Bow and Setup

Any bow and bow setup a hunter would use for white-tailed deer will work well for turkeys. Some bowhunters advocate reducing draw weight for hunting turkeys. The reasoning is that the range is short, penetration is not a problem, and the need often arises to hold at full draw for long periods. This is true for hunters not using blinds, and I would agree that those hunters would do well to reduce their draw weight to a comfortable level. For those hunters in blinds, this is not an issue. I prefer not to change my draw weight back and forth between seasons, since this usually requires retuning the bow, may require use of a different arrow, and always requires adjustments and additional practice on my part. Better for those using blinds (assuming they also hunt deer or other game with their bows) to tune their bows to one draw weight and stick with it.

The fact that turkeys can see color is something to consider. Most hunters prefer brightly colored fletching and nocks, since these make it easier to see hits and to locate arrows. These work fine for color-blind big game animals, but a quiver full of brightly colored arrows is probably not a good idea for turkey hunting. Furthermore, there is the safety issue. Turkey hunters are frequently advised to avoid wearing red, white, or blue in the turkey woods, since these are the colors of a gobbler's head. Even if the hunter plans to use a blind, he will be hiking to and from the hunting spot, and may find himself searching for a bird that has been hit but not anchored to the spot. A few arrows with green, brown, or black fletching are worth the trouble or the expense.

Decoys

Some bowhunters advocate using decoys religiously. The usually recommended setup entails a hen or jake facing the hunter, and the idea is that the gobbler will circle the decoy to display, thereby facing away from the hunter in full strut, giving the bowhunter the opportunity to draw. This is another of those points that becomes almost moot with the use of a blind, but the bowhunter who insists on hunting in the open would do well to carry a decoy or two. They don't always work, but the bowhunter needs every edge he can get.

I usually put out two hens and a jake when I bowhunt. I've observed several reactions. The most common reaction is no reaction at all. On a recent hunt an Eastern gobbler strutted past two hen decoys, a jake decoy, and two live hens to come within yards of my blind. I was clucking and purring on a Hunter's Tech diaphragm call (two-time World Turkey Calling Champion caller Larry Norton makes them in Alabama), and I can only believe that the gobbler was keying in on the calls, and was less interested in the visible but non-vocal birds.

Sometimes gobblers do react to decoys, displaying and approaching from long distances across meadows, for instance. I believe they may react indirectly, too - the decoys can give them confidence to approach a caller more closely than they might otherwise.

On the other hand, I have seen gobblers react negatively to decoys. A less-than dominant gobbler may shy away from them for fear of being caught by the boss. And a decoy that spins in the wind, falls over, or behaves in any other unnatural way can spook any turkey. It's important to take the time to set decoys up properly. A stick a few inches from either side of the tail will allow the bird to move a little, but not to spin around.

Some movement is good - a gobbler that doesn't react to decoys sometimes becomes very interested if he detects movement. There are decoys - Flambeau's Motion Hen is one I've used to good effect - designed to move. The Motion Hen is set up with a string that runs to the hunter, so that a slight tug on the string makes the decoy's head bob downward in a way that simulates a feeding hen. Other decoys are battery operated, and these work well where legal. The downside to these decoys is their weight and lack of portability. I use them only when hunting from a blind, and then only when I have a short hike or drive to my blind.

Because I almost invariably hunt from a blind when I bowhunt turkeys, I put the decoys close - usually inside ten yards. I typically set up on the edge of a meadow, where I can see for a long distance. In other setups, safety must be taken into account. Avoid setups that would put you in the line of fire if another hunter should shoot at your decoys.

Where To Shoot

If the turkey is facing you, aim at the spot where the beard emerges from the breast. If the turkey is facing away from you in full strut, try to put the arrow right up his vent. If he is standing erect, facing away, shoot right through his middle to spine him.

Call maker and world champion caller Larry Norton with a gobbler at Alabama's Bent Creek Lodge.

On a broadside shot, there are two schools of thinking. Conventional wisdom says aim for the wing butt, where the vitals are and close to the spine. Increasing numbers of bowhunters suggest aiming just above the legs. A broken hip will put the bird down for keeps. If the shot is a little low, a broken leg will accomplish the same thing. A little high, and there is a good chance of spining the gobbler. I can't speak for the leg shot from personal experience, having never intentionally done it. I can confirm that if a turkey's leg is broken, he can neither run nor get off the ground to fly.

Full strut broadside shots are difficult. It's hard to tell where the vitals or the spine are when the gobbler is all puffed up, and the illusion of a bigger target is created. Better to cluck or whistle to bring the bird out of full strut, then shoot. Sometimes gobblers won't come out of full strut. In that case, hold well above center on the forward part of the wing.

Practice and More

In gun hunting, pulling the trigger is usually anticlimactic. Not so with bowhunting. Everything can be exactly right, but the bowhunter must still make the shot to collect his trophy, and that is never a given. Practicing on 3D turkey targets is an exercise well worthwhile. It's also important to practice shooting from any position you might shoot from while turkey hunting. If you'll be sitting or kneeling on the ground, practice that shot. If you'll be sitting on a bucket or in a chair, practice from that very bucket or chair if possible. Practice shooting from your blind. Make sure the shooting ports are at the right height for whatever positions you'll be shooting from. If you plan to use a string tracker, tune your bow and shoot withthe tracker on the bow. You'll want to take at least a few shots with the string attached to your arrows.

Practice at least a few times wearing all your turkey hunting clothing. I find, for instance, that I must adjust my release aid to accommodate my camo gloves. I've also discovered that some headnets will invariably get in the way of my bowstring. Making these discoveries at a backyard practice session is fine; making them when you've finally gotten that big gobbler in range will ruin your whole weekend.

Bowhunting turkeys will always be a challenge. By taking advantage of every edge he can get in the way of the best blinds, broadheads, decoys, rangefinders, and other gear, and by leaving as little as possible to chance by scouting thoroughly, selecting setups carefully, and practice shooting regularly, the bowhunter can make the odds against success much less daunting than they will otherwise be. The wait for success may be longer, the need for patience and discipline higher, and the frustrations more frequent, but that only makes success all the sweeter for the bowhunter. Take a gobbler with a bow and you will have joined an elite fraternity among hunters.

Note: Bowhunters who may be interested in making fletching from the feathers of wild turkeys they harvest should see Chapter 19: The Trophy.

Modern bowhunters have a few advantages. A Seminole with authentic traditional clothing and equipment draws his bow. Note the rattlesnake bow cover.

Tips

• Wear shooting glasses to increase contrast in the woods.

• Laser rangefinders are good investments for turkey hunters. Pick out several strategic landmarks when you set up, and determine their range, in effect establishing a perimeter inside which you will pull the trigger at the first good opportunity. Working a turkey is a test of wills, patience, and judgment; eliminating distractions and nagging worries about range enables you to hunt with more confidence.

• In fields, turkeys like to stand behind low, rolling hills, over which they raise their heads like a periscope, motionless, and survey the landscape for danger. Mixed in with a few stalks of grass, their exposed heads and necks are very difficult to see.

• Approach openings very carefully and glass them thoroughly before setting up.

"But what was merely recreation to the rest of my family was the very breath of life to me. When I was little more than a baby I used to toddle after my father to pick up his cartridge cases after he fired and sniff the delicious odor of gunpowder that clung to them."

--J. A. Hunter, Hunter, 1952

Chapter 9

OPTICS
FOR TURKEY HUNTERS

A few years ago I told a friend that middle age was coming at me like a freight train. Not long after that I took a youngster on his first turkey hunt, and the sad truth was evident: that train had already flattened me. You see, the kid was pointing out turkeys to me. Me! He not only spotted them before I did, he distinguished gobblers from jakes and compared beard lengths and body sizes at distances that had me reaching for my binoculars to be certain I was looking at turkeys. I hadn't realized how vain I was about my vision and my ability to spot game, and the evidence of my impending decrepitude didn't brighten my day. The fact is, though, I became a better turkey hunter after that, because the realization forced me to rely more heavily on binoculars. Every serious turkey hunter should invest in quality binoculars and use them, for the simple reason that no human's eyes are a match for those of the wild turkey.

Unless a hunter is sitting motionless, turkeys will see him first nineteen times out of twenty. Those odds can be improved somewhat by hunters who use extreme stealth, taking careful advantage of cover and the terrain, who know the lay of the land, and who use good binoculars.

Using and Selecting Binoculars

Turkey hunting is a paraphernalia-intensive endeavor. We make our way through the woods with an assortment of calls, decoys, gun and ammunition, canteen, snack, bug dope, headnet, seat pad, and various other assorted items. Who can blame turkey hunters for preferring compact binoculars to full-sized ones? Ideally, you should have a full-sized pair and a compact pair. There is no denying the advantages of full-sized binoculars in terms of light-gathering capabilities and field of view. You'll use them for pre-season scouting, if not for actual hunting. If two pair of quality binoculars aren't in the budget, a pair of decent compacts will do. Quality optics are not cheap, but almost any binoculars are better than none.

Full size binoculars are ideal for scouting. For hunting, most hunters prefer a good pair of compact binoculars.

The key word there is "almost." If the lenses aren't properly aligned, you'll find you're not using them because trying to get a single sharp image is frustrating and can cause headaches. Also, if condensation steams them up every time you use them, or if a mechanical problem makes them impossible to focus, whatever small amount of money they cost was money wasted.

On the other hand, turkey hunters can find some very good compact binoculars on the market for less than what they'll pay for a new shotgun. Finding them is not that tough if you know what you want and are willing to do a little comparison shopping. You needn't research the technical aspects of optics to compare the performance of one pair of binoculars with another. Most hunters understand power of magnification, and many place too much emphasis on it. A good, bright, crisp pair of 7X binoculars is far better than a pair of not-so-crisp, not-so-bright 8X binoculars, and will probably be brighter and have a larger field of view. Field of view is important when you're scanning a big meadow for turkeys, or when you've spotted something in the distance and need to put the glasses on it in a hurry. Higher power binoculars are generally not ideal for turkey hunters, since these are difficult to hold steady without a tripod or other rest of some sort. The best image in the world is of little use if it's bouncing around uncontrollably.

The brightness of binoculars, or the amount of light admitted, is influenced by several things, but is determined mostly by the size of the exit pupil, which is the size of the objective, or forward, lens, divided by the magnification of the binoculars. A pair of 7X35 binoculars has an exit pupil of five. Up to a point, the bigger the exit pupil, the brighter the lens. Brightness isn't everything in binoculars, but it's important, not only in the low light of early morning and late afternoon, but in a dense forest, or when looking into a shaded area. Clearly compact lens, with their much smaller objective lens, cannot compete with full-sized lenses in terms of brightness.

How important are waterproof binoculars? If you frequently hunt around water, carrying the binoculars in a boat, or if you often hunt swamps, the extra money spent for waterproof binoculars may be a good investment. You will pay considerably more for waterproof binoculars than for the non-waterproof version of the same model. Most hunters would probably do better to save the money, or put it into better glass. Porro-prisms or roof-prism binoculars? The difference is distinguishable at a glance; porro prisms have the traditional dog-leg in the barrels, roof prism binoculars are straight. Certainly there are some outstanding roof-prism binoculars on the market, and these should not be ruled out. The old rule of thumb, though, which still applies to most binoculars, is that a pair of roof prisms will be more expensive than a pair of porro-prisms of comparable quality. In other words, porro-prisms usually offer more for the money. Comparing the quality of the glass, or the resolution, is not that difficult. Ultimately this will come down to looking through numerous binoculars side-by-side, in the same spot, but you can winnow out some models by looking for a few advertised features. BaK-4 glass is a standard of quality that is often advertised, and an indication of good, sharp lenses. Most binoculars feature "coated lenses," or "multi-coated lenses," but the best usuallyoffer fully coated lenses, and will say so. Coated lenses can brighten as well as sharpen the image.

When you've identified all the features you want and selected some models in your price range to compare, find something in the distance--a printed sign is good--and look at the sign through each pair of binoculars. You'll probably be surprised at the differences in sharpness from one pair of similarly-priced binoculars to another. Naturally, the more binoculars you look through, the more confidence you'll have that you're buying the best you can get for the money.

Rangefinders

If I was slow to catch on to the importance of binoculars, there is one optical device I haven't hit the spring turkey woods without for as long as they've been available: laser rangefinders. I don't know how many turkey hunters are above the temptation to push the range limits of their shotgun, but any hunter who has ever sat pinned down for an hour or more by a tom strutting just out of range, arm tiring from holding the gun in position, a tree knot digging into the back, a root making the butt numb, and a bug humming under the facenet, can understand the temptation. Add to that honest errors in judging distance, and there is little doubt that most turkey hunters could benefit greatly from the use of a good rangefinder.

Even the most patient and cautious turkey hunter will find rangefinders beneficial. By setting up and ranging on several prominent landmarks, the hunter can in effect form a shooting perimeter at the maximum effective range of his shotgun, beyond which he will not shoot, inside of which he will pull the trigger at the very first opportunity. This inspires confidence, and leaves the hunter free to concentrate on calling strategies and the bird itself, without the distraction of worrying about when to shoot. Ranging on an approaching turkey is not practical, and there will be occasions when the rangefinder cannot be used at all; in most instances, though, ranging on a few landmarks immediately after setting up takes only a few seconds.

I have several of the old-style split-screen rangefinders. I find them slow and not precise enough to be useful, but that could be a reflection of my poor vision and a lack of practice using them. If you have a pair and have confidence in it, these might be all you need.

Laser rangefinders are worthwhile investments for the turkey hunter. Readouts are instant and precise in most situations.

Laser rangefinders, such as those made by Bushnell, Nikon, and Leica, are fast and reliable. I use them for turkey hunting, bowhunting in general, and black-powder hunting. Since few individuals have any business shooting centerfire rifles at ranges beyond about 200 yards in hunting situations, I'm somewhat mystified by the drive toward increasingly powerful rangefinders that reach to 600, 800, and 1000 yards. Laser rangefinders are marketed to golfers as well as hunters, and knowing more about golf than I want to (which is a tiny bit more than nothing), I can only assume it is the golfers who demand increasingly powerful rangefinders. (This has a plus side - "obsolete" rangefinders that reach only to 400 or 600 yards can often be purchased inexpensively from golfers eager for the newest and most powerful model. Look under golfing accessories on any on-line auction.)

Optical Sights

I've not yet made the switch to telescopic sights, but they are probably in my future. Aging eyes have increasing difficulty focusing on iron sights, but it isn't just a matter of age. Any hunter whose vision requires more than a slight correction can probably benefit from telescopic, holographic, or red dot sights. Any turkey hunter who misses birds on more than the rare occasion should probably consider optical sights. In the excitement of the moment, many hunters are so focused on the target that they fail to put their heads down with their cheeks against the stock. Without realizing it, they look over the barrel instead of down the barrel, often missing by wide margins.

Optical sights tend to encourage concentration and force hunters to take careful aim. Telescopic sights for turkey hunting are typically in the 1.5-4X range, with a wide field of view for quick target acquisition. Many shotguns aimed at the turkey hunting market come drilled and tapped for scopes, but special shotgun scope mounts that require no drilling are available at sporting-goods stores or at catalog companies such as Cabela's, Redhead, NightLite, and others.

There is a safety argument that favors telescopic sights, and it may have some merit. The mature, responsible hunter identifies his target without regard to the kind of sights he uses, but anything that increases concentration and encourages careful target identification among youthful or excitable hunters is a good thing. One concern associated with telescopic sights is that any degree of magnification may cause a hunter to underestimate range and take long shots. There is some merit to that argument, too, and those using scoped shotguns should take steps to avoid being fooled by even a 1.5X scope. Some hunters avoid this problem by using see-through scope mounts, which enable them to look down the barrel under the scope until they are ready to shoot, at which point they raise their heads slightly to look through the scope.

Red dot and holographic sights are increasing in popularity, and offer similar advantages of a wide field of view, quick target acquisition, and minute-of-angle precision. Regardless of the position of the shooter's head, if the gun has been sighted in and the dot is on the target, the pattern will center there. These sights also tend to be compact and light in weight.

The chief argument against optical sights for turkey hunting is the comparative lack of simplicity. Properly installed and sighted in, a good scope will stay on target. A good scope will not be damaged by the recoil from a magnum shotshell. Good scopes shouldn't fog up, at least internally. But the scope has not yet been designed that has never jarred loose, never been damaged by recoil, or never fogged up. The risk is slight in the case of quality optics, but is any risk worth it? For those whose vision is not excellent, or for those who get excited and tend not to put their cheeks against the stock, or worse yet, fail to identify the target carefully, the answer is probably yes. For others, it's a close call.

Quality optics are useful tools for any turkey hunter. Are they essential? I don't use a scope, and I killed quite a few turkeys before I began using binoculars or laser rangefinders. On the other hand, I'd hate to give up my optics now that I've grown accustomed to using them. Picking between my binoculars and my rangefinder would be tough, if I had to make that decision, though overall, binoculars strike me as the most useful optical tool for a turkey hunter, should he be limited to one. I know hunters who use telescopic or red dot scopes who will never return to open sights, and certainly these can be essential items for some hunters. Ultimately, there is no doubt in my mind that quality optics can give hunters an extra edge and add enjoyment to their hunt.

"Turkeys can fly only a short distance, so those that fly away can be easily located and stalked a second or even third time."

--Len McDougall
Practical Outdoor Survival,1992

Chapter 10

RECOVERING TURKEYS

Those of us who lack Mr. McDougall's astonishing skills find locating and successfully stalking a wild turkey that we have flushed a decidedly low-percentage undertaking. Most turkey hunters won't attempt it, and I don't blame them.

Anchor him with a second shot if you can; if not, don't chase. A wounded turkey will usually travel in a straight line, and will seek cover quickly if not pursued. Wait 30 minutes or more, then begin a methodical search.

Recovering a wounded turkey, though, is another matter. It's not easy, mind you, and is never a sure thing. Turkeys leave no blood trail to speak of, and cannot be tracked, except in snow, for any distance. On the other hand, locating a wounded turkey does not require supernatural powers. In fact, the odds of success for the diligent hunter are much greater than you might think.

The need to locate a wounded turkey should be a fairly rare occurrence. The ethical hunter has patterned his gun and shoots only when the target is positively identified, is within range, is clear of other turkeys, and offers a reasonably good shot. Still, the quickness of the turkey, the human propensity to choke under pressure, and just plain bad luck make it possible for even the most conscientious hunter to find himself in the disheartening position of having a turkey run (or fly) off after a shot.

Most clean misses occur at close range. It is very easy to miss a turkey at close range, since the shot pattern is small, perhaps the size of a softball. At thirty yards or more your pattern may be the size of a car door; if the turkey runs or flies off at that distance, the chances are very good that you put at least a few shot into the bird. Turkeys are tough, though, and even a lot of shot may not bring them down quickly if the brain or spine is not hit.

Quick action can head off potential problems. It is not unusual for a turkey to be momentarily stunned, only to regain its feet and escape as an overconfident hunter ambles over to collect his trophy. The proper response after shooting a turkey with a shotgun is to push the safety on and hurry to the bird with gun at the ready. As long as the turkey's head is on the ground, the hunter should continue moving quickly toward the bird. If its head comes up, the hunter should stop, take aim, and shoot again.

A clean kill with a single shot is the best way to insure recovery. "Dead" turkeys occasionally run off, so push on the safe and hurry to the bird with gun at the ready.

Upon reaching the bird, whether or not a second shot is necessary, beginning hunters do well to follow the time-tested tradition of standing on its head or neck until it stops thrashing and relaxes. It's easy to get careless after you've bagged a few birds, but watch those spurs! More experienced hunters, in part to prevent the bird from breaking or bending tail or wing feathers as it thrashes, may instead immediately grab the turkey by the legs and lift it from the ground. The trick is to do it decisively, grabbing both legs simultaneously above the spurs. A turkey with a broken leg cannot run, and normally cannot get off the ground to fly. Save a shell if you must, but shooting the bird again is probably the quickest and surest way to dispatch it.

What might seem obvious when contemplated from a detached situation is often overlooked in the excitement of the hunt, so I will state the obvious: Watch the bird as far as you can see it, and when you can no longer see it listen carefully for as long as you can hear it. On a hunt in South Texas, I once made a poor shot at a Rio Grande that rose straight into the air and flew off. The bird suddenly dropped like a stone and hit the ground with an audible thud. It took me awhile to find that gobbler, partly because I was in thick blackbrush country, but mostly because I had underestimated the distance at which he fell--I thought it to be about sixty yards, but later paced it off at 110 yards. My point is that I easily heard the big bird hit the ground from 110 yards away.

Turkeys, like upland game birds, will sometimes fly off or run off only to drop dead at some distance. Listen for the sound of the bird hitting the ground or thrashing after it is out of sight.

A turkey plummeting through the trees, or attempting unsuccessfully to land in them, usually makes even more noise. Whether the bird is flying or running, anything you can do to get a line on it will greatly increase your chances of recovering it. Make no mistake, most wounded game, turkeys included, can be recovered by hunters who think before they act and who are diligent in pursuit of their quarry. Wounded turkeys tend to travel in a straight line, though they often take the line of least resistance, and they will seek cover within 200 yards, usually less.

After you have watched and listened to the bird leave the area, take careful note of the position from which you shot, and the spot where the bird was standing when hit, before you do anything else. A compass can be invaluable here, especially in areas where foliage is thick, or in hill country. Walking in a straight line is beyond the ability of the most accomplished woodsman when visibility is limited.

Over the years I've become convinced that the best procedure, once all positions are marked, is to wait at least twenty minutes before setting out after the bird. Even a hard-hit bird can cover a lot of ground if hotly pursued. If not hotly pursued, on the other hand, a wounded bird will not travel far before seeking cover. After waiting, move quietly but deliberately in the direction you believe the turkey took. Look for a red or white head in the woods. Search carefully in every blowdown, a favorite hiding place for wounded game of any kind. Check out drainages. Look in creek bottoms, especially under the roots of trees along the banks. Small thickets should be explored carefully. Occasionally, a hard-hit bird will simply huddle against a stump or large rock.

If you spot the bird from a distance, don't walk directly toward it. If it believes it has been spotted, it may run or fly again. Instead, walk at an angle to the bird. Some hunters go a step further and avoid looking directly at the turkey, since the birds can recognize eye contact. You may very well recover the turkey by walking directly toward it, staring intently at it all the while. Still, there is no downside I can think of to walking at an angle or avoiding eye contact with a wounded turkey, and I believe it can reduce the likelihood of the bird's bolting off through the woods. However you approach the bird, as soon as you are comfortably within shotgun range, stop, take aim, and shoot.

You often won't spot a turkey in a blowdown or undercut bank until you're right on top of it. You'll have to use your judgment, depending on the circumstances, as to how best to dispatch the bird. If the turkey's head is up and he seems alert, and if the cover is not too thick to prevent it, by all means back off and shoot again. The last thing you want to do is find yourself blazing away at a turkey running through the woods. Turkeys can run thirty miles an hour - no easy target bobbing and weaving through the tree trunks. If you hit it at close range you may spoil some meat. And if you miss, you will be faced with starting all over again on a search that could easily have been ended.

Bowhunting Problems

The situation is different for bowhunters. As an avid bowhunter, I'm well aware of how lethal a sharp broadhead can be on any game animal. The vital zone on a turkey is small, though, and unless you spine the bird or make a head shot, there is a good chance he will run or fly some distance before collapsing. In my video library is footage of a gobbler flying over the treetops with an arrow through his chest. (Also on video, happily, is the recovery of that bird. Unfortunately, what is not on video is the priceless expression of the bowhunter watching in disbelief as the turkey flies away with his arrow through it.)

One item that can help prevent crippling losses for bowhunters is a mechanical, or open-on-impact, broadhead. Though I remain skeptical about their effectiveness on most big game, they are ideal for turkeys. Good ones do indeed fly like field points, and given the relatively small size of a turkey's vitals, accuracy is paramount. At the same time, the larger heads expand to a diameter of two inches or more, punching quite a hole and greatly increasing the chance of hitting vitals, spining the bird, or breaking a leg, any of which virtually assures recovery. The chief knock against mechanical heads is that they impede penetration. This is not a problem for turkey hunters, many of whom intentionally impede penetration with stoppers of various sorts. I'm not convinced this is necessary but, in any case, penetration is not something turkey hunters normally need to worry about.

String trackers can help bowhunters recover turkeys.

Another item that can improve the chance for recovery is the string tracker. Some bowhunters wouldn't think of hunting turkeys without one. Any impact on accuracy out to twenty-five yards (some claim thirty) is slight. The fact is, very few if any bowhunters should be shooting at turkeys beyond twenty-five yards, and the majority should limit their range to twenty yards or less.

Critics of string trackers like to point out that they do not guarantee recovery. That is true. Neither does any other method or accessory I'm aware of. The string can break. It doesn't, usually, but if it does, the hunter is no worse off than any other hunter who goes afield without one in the first place. String trackers do present a few disadvantages: They add weight to the bow, and the string can get caught on limbs or in grass when the bowhunter is moving. Whether or not the disadvantages outweigh the advantages is a personal decision, but anyone who goes after turkeys with a bow owes it to himself and his quarry to give string trackers a try.

In looking for an arrowed turkey that has run or flown off, all the previous suggestions for gun hunters apply. If using a string tracker, proceed cautiously and quietly, looking ahead for the end of the string. Keep an arrow nocked. When a bowhunter spots the crippled bird, he should slip to within a comfortable range, stop, and put another arrow into the bird. Don't rush the shot, but don't delay it, either. Draw, aim, and release smoothly. Clearly, it is even more important for the bowhunter than for the gun hunter that the bird not break and run. Unless the hunter is very unlucky, a second arrow through the bird will anchor it.

Whether gun hunting or bowhunting, it's important not to give up easily on a wounded turkey. Keep in mind that a wounded turkey rarely goes much farther than 200 yards, and a hard-hit bird will not go that far. Search all cover methodically before giving up. Perseverance usually pays off.

The walk out can be a long one with a heavy longbeard over the shoulder - but it's even longer if you leave an unrecovered bird in the woods.

"My grown son still does not hunt, and still I wonder what he's missed and what his children will miss. Will animals be mere sentimental abstractions? Curiosities in the landscape? It worries me."

--Aldo Leopold
Aldo Leopold's Southwest, 1944

Chapter 11

GUIDING

I nearly jumped out of my skin when a gobbler exploded from the top of a cedar tree directly over our heads, sending a shower of twigs down around us, and flew off over the hill we were climbing.

"Wow!" I said, turning to my friend. "Did you see the beard on that gobbler?"

"What gobbler?"

"You're telling me you didn't see or hear that big gobbler that just flew over our heads?"

We'll call my friend Jim, and his blank stare told me all I needed to know, though the rest of the morning confirmed it. Jim wouldn't see a gobbler if it wasn't standing in the open at close range, and wouldn't hear it unless it gobbled in his ear. And neither of those things was likely to happen, because Jim couldn't sit still long enough to let a turkey get that close. Since that day I've guided a number of "Jims." It's usually evident very early in the hunt, and believe me it's a long day when you realize the hunter you are guiding is extremely unlikely to fill his tag no matter what you do. Every turkey hunting guide has been there.

On the other hand, I've guided some excellent hunters to their first turkeys, too, and that is every bit as rewarding as you might imagine it to be. Most turkey hunters eventually become guides - not in the professional sense, of course, but in the sense of occasionally taking a youngster or a beginning turkey hunter out to get them started and perhaps call in a turkey for them. It can be immensely rewarding, and it can be among the more difficult and frustrating experiences of your life, depending in part on the individual for whom you are guiding, and probably in equal measure on your own temperament.

Guiding Children

Kids aren't one size fits all. They come in two genders, all shapes and sizes, and they cover a wide range of ages. But though they differ in a number of particulars, there are a few things they tend to have in common. One is that, given a chance, virtually all of them enjoy being outdoors and discovering nature. When they don't, it's usually because adults have done something to ruin it for them. Sometimes, in our enthusiasm to instill in them our love for hunting and the outdoors, we forget a couple of very basic things.

Turkey hunting is a great way to introduce kids to the outdoors.

First, we sometimes forget they lack our strength and endurance. Kids take two or three steps for every one of ours. Unless the youngster in question is an athletic teenager, we're making a mistake if we plan on hiking the hills and covering a lot of ground. Take it easy. If you've got to hunt big hill country, hunt an area where driving to the top is an option. Don't plan to walk more than a mile or so, and take your time doing it. Hunt a good spot or two from which you can bring the birds to you.

Second, we forget that kids as a rule lack the focus and the patience of adults. A gobbler that is sounding off or putting on a show will hold their attention for a while. Apart from that, they're going to get bored in thirty to sixty minutes. It's not their responsibility to stay interested, it's ours to make things interesting.

Keeping Kids Involved

Kids will quickly get tired of just tagging along. Who wouldn't? Giving them things to do is easy, and makes them feel they are contributing to the hunt. Give them a locator call or two, and let them use it. Any loud sound that isn't obviously of human origin can make a turkey shock gobble. My ten-year-old daughter loves to squawk on a crow call.

Even kids not ready to shoot can do a lot in the turkey woods. They can call, to begin with, and they can read sign.

The crows often answer, and sometimes I let her keep squawking until some crows are circling overhead and landing in the trees nearby. She gets a huge kick out of talking to the crows. If a gobbler responds, she's thrilled, and feels that she's part of the hunt - which, of course, she is.

And don't think kids can't call in turkeys. Those little push-pin box calls on the market are virtually foolproof, and kids can learn in a matter of minutes to yelp and cluck on them well enough to call in a turkey.

Kids can carry gear, too. Let them carry a pair of inexpensive compact binoculars, and use them. They can carry decoys. I sometimes carry a Flambeau Motion Hen when hunting with kids. A string runs from the decoy to the hunter, to make the decoy's head bob in simulation of feeding. Operating the decoy is the kid's job.

Kids' hearing is usually better than that of adults. Before calling to locate a bird, my daughter and I stand at least ten feet apart, so the sounds of breathing, clothes rustling, and so forth, aren't a factor. She knows her hearing is better than mine is, and it makes her feel important that I rely on her to hear distant gobblers.

Take Breaks

Take a snack break at least once, maybe twice in the course of a morning's hunt. And be prepared to forget about turkey hunting altogether now and then. I caution my kids not to talk, but they're allowed to whisper. A whisper won't carry far, and I have some doubts that a turkey recognizes a whisper even when it hears one. We examine turkey feathers, count the box turtles we see, examine turkey, deer, and other tracks, identify the birds we hear, and at least once in the course of a hunt we're going to end up just playing in the creek, looking for fish and crawdads and snake skins and probably getting wet. Knock off early. Don't wait until the kid is tired and hot and whining and complaining - far better to leave while you're both still having fun.

A Secret Weapon for Kids

Kids don't necessarily need to see a filled tag to get hooked on turkey hunting, but sooner or later they do need to see turkeys. Chances are if they get a good look at a gobbler in full strut, they'll be hooked. The problem is that few kids can sit motionless long enough to let a turkey get close enough to be really observed, let alone within shotgun range.

The solution to the problem is as simple as a blind. (See Chapter 8 for a more in-depth discussion of hunting blinds.) In a blind, kids can sit comfortably on a chair or stool and fidget as much as they like so long as they don't make noise. They can even talk occasionally, if they keep it to a whisper. When a turkey comes in, they can observe all the action. Watching jakes and hens interact is enjoyable and will hold their attention for long periods, in addition to being educational. The only thing most kids need to be cautioned about is putting their face or their hands right up to the openings in the blind. They all want to do it, and it will defeat the purpose of the blind.

Unless it's an unusually busy day, with birds in sight much of the time, there is a limit to how long a kid will stay in a blind. When hunting with most kids, I've settled into a routine that entails staying in the blind for an hour and a half or two hours after fly-down time, then leaving the blind for a break. That's when we take a little walk, find some turtles or mushrooms, play in a creek, have a snack. Then, after half an hour or an hour, we head back to the blind for another session.

The newer, more portable, quick set-up blinds offer the advantage of greater mobility, but it is difficult with most kids to move quickly and quietly through the woods to set up for, and relocate on, gobblers. The key is to locate strutting areas or travel lanes such as forest openings, ridgetop trails, logging roads, and so forth, and work turkeys from these. Large meadows and pastures are ideal, because not only do turkeys usually gravitate to these, but they offer high visibility. In these areas, kids get to watch turkeys come in from long distances. With any luck, they'll see gobblers in full strut. And even if the turkeys are at a distance and won't respond to calling or to decoys, kids find it exciting to see them and watch them.

Hunting With Kids

So far we've been assuming the kid you're guiding is not yet ready to carry a gun and fill a tag himself. Turkey hunting is an ideal way to introduce kids to hunting for several reasons.

First, it's almost always a one-on-one situation. Almost any form of hunting can be one-on-one, of course, but turkey hunting lends itself readily to that style of hunting.

Second, shooting at a turkey is normally a one-shot, very controlled situation. The approach of a gobbler is exciting, but doesn't typically startle a kid the way the flush of an upland bird does, nor does it call for a quick reaction. There is almost always time to observe, prepare, and think about one deliberate shot.

The smile says better than I can why it's important to take kids hunting.

Third, the shot can and usually should be coached. Gobblers rarely if ever react to quiet whispers (assuming they can even hear them), or the guide can use a pre-arranged signal to shoot. It's difficult to imagine a safer shooting situation than one in which a parent or other adult guide will be sitting beside or immediately behind a youngster, indicating when it's safe and appropriate to shoot, and reminding them to put the safety on or to open the action after shooting and before hurrying to the target.

My "clients" have invariably thanked me after a successful hunt-and I've invariably felt it was I who owed them the thanks, for the privilege of sharing the experience.

Guiding Adults

Guiding adults is naturally very different from guiding youngsters, but the goal is much the same: to recruit a turkey hunter into the sport, and to teach him or her a little about turkey hunting in the process. Some of the caveats about kids shouldn't apply to adults, but we do strive for a successful hunt, which means the hunt should be enjoyable whether or not we drive away with a turkey in the back of the vehicle.

That starts with a clear understanding of our "client's" abilities. How old is he or she, and what is his or her physical condition? What kind of hunting experience does he or she have? Chances are any big-game hunter understands the importance of being quiet and keeping motion to a minimum, but the same is not true for the hunter who has hunted only upland game. I hunt upland game over pointing dogs, and love it dearly, but let's face it: Hunting upland game behind a dog has more to do with dog training and handling, hiking vigorously (or not so vigorously), and wingshooting, than it does with "hunting." The upland game hunter may be inclined to talk, walk through sunny openings instead of instinctively sticking to cover and shadows, and see and hear only what is obvious and close by. I find that most beginning turkey hunters need to be cautioned now and then to remain as motionless as possible when sitting still, and to be as quiet as possible when moving.

It amazes me that many turkey hunters will head afield having never patterned their guns. Here the beginner may have the excuse of ignorance. In any case, try to determine if your hunter has patterned his gun. If a hunter I'm guiding has not patterned his gun, I encourage him to use mine. If that doesn't work, I explain that we will have to limit our shots to close range-usually twenty-five yards, depending on the gun, the load, and how it is choked.

It is essential that the guide be able to communicate quickly and quietly with the hunter. Establish a few simple auditory or hand signals. If you are not confident of the hunter's ability to distinguish a gobbler from a hen, for instance, you'll want a way to signal that information.

If the hunter has some experience, and is simply interested in learning a little more about calling and hunting strategies, some tactics can be used that might not be practical with a less-experienced hunter. For instance, you needn't set up beside or immediately behind the more experienced hunter, and in many cases shouldn't. It can be helpful to call from a position twenty, thirty, or more yards behind the hunter, so that a gobbler that hangs up will be within shooting range. (The risk in this is that if a bird comes in from an unexpected direction, the hunter will not be in a position to shoot.) In some cases, when a bird hangs up, the guide can move away from the gobbler, calling all the while. This sometimes makes the gobbler think the hen is leaving, and may entice a hung-up bird to move toward the "hen" and past the shooter.

The less-experienced hunter will benefit more from the nearby presence of the guide, who can communicate what's going on, encourage patience, tell him when to get the gun in position and when to shoot, and so on.

As I indicated in Chapter 6, blinds can be useful for hunting with adults as well as with youngsters, for the simple reason that two hunters make twice the noise and commotion as one, and constantly experience the temptation and sometimes the need to communicate with one another by talking or gesturing. Remember my hopeless friend Jim, who didn't see or hear the gobbler that flew off the roost right over our heads? I'm not sure if this argues for or against blinds for turkey hunting, but the season after Jim's first hunt, I set up a blind at one end of a pasture where I had frequently seen gobblers strutting, and guaranteed him that if he would spend three mornings sitting in that blind, he'd get a shot at a gobbler. The second morning a lone gobbler walked within thirty yards of the blind and Jim killed his first turkey.

A Point About Safety

There is no reason to think that two people hunting together is unsafe, but there is no denying the added potential for accidents when two hunters travel together, especially when one of them is a beginner. A few precautions are in order.

The moment when the trigger is pulled and the bird goes down might be the most potentially hazardous. Turkey hunters are accustomed to hurrying to the turkey and pinning it to the ground, or lifting it off the ground to prevent damage to tail or wing feathers. Never get in front of the shooter. In the unlikely event the bird regains its feet, you aren't going to catch it. The best chance for recovery is to remain behind the shooter, who can then shoot again. Don't worry about a few bent tail feathers in this situation. Wait until you're sure the bird is down, then accompany the shooter to the bird, reminding him if necessary to put on the safety and open the action.

Thanks to the efforts of turkey hunters, the National Wild Turkey Federation, and the various state divisions of wildlife, turkey-hunting accidents are declining. Nevertheless, diligence about hunting safety issues is always in order. Less-experienced turkey hunters should always be reminded to use caution when calling. Using gobbler calls should be discouraged except in certain circumstances. (Some would say in any circumstances.) Hunters should use extra caution when using decoys. And though locating gobblers and moving in close to them is part of the game, attempting to stalk within gun range of a gobbler is not usually a good idea.

This father and son will never forget the days they spent turkey hunting together.

"I don't believe all turkey hunters will agree on any one subject pertaining to the wild turkey. That's good. It proves that the wild turkey has been, to a marked degree, successful in addling the brain of the people who pursue himwith uncertainty."

--Gene Nunnery
The Old Pro Turkey Hunter, 1980

Chapter 12

THE OPTIMUM TURKEY GUN

While much depends on the individual hunter, it can be a useful exercise to explore the attributes that a good turkey gun should possess. Some of these are very subjective factors, but even the less subjective qualities are open to some debate. Length, for instance, is a measurable, objective quality. The conventional thinking is that short-barreled shotguns--say twenty-six-inch barrels or shorter -- are preferable for turkey hunting. The turkey hunter must often swing his gun slowly to track an approaching bird, and must occasionally change positions quickly to move the barrel from, say, the 2 o'clock position to the 9 o'clock position when a gobbler sneaks in from an unexpected direction. It's amazing how often a tree, a low-hanging limb, or a shrub of some kind obstructs that movement, preventing a shot or requiring exaggerated movements that risk spooking the target. It's even more amazing how often a barrel just two or three inches shorter would eliminate the problem.

On the other hand, some very accomplished turkey hunters prefer longer barrels. Why? The longer sight plane makes for more accurate shooting, which is important for tightly choked barrels sending small patterns at a target the size of a turkey's head. As for obstructions getting in the way, say these hunters, that's what pruning shears are for. For my own part, I find the arguments in favor of shorter barrels more persuasive. To the extent that accuracy is a problem, a low-power scope, or even good iron sights, will better resolve the problem, and without the extra weight and length.

Is gauge really a point of debate? My friend and fellow outdoor writer Tony Mandile has taken several turkeys I know of with a 20-gauge O/U. No doubt the old saw 'Beware the one-gun man' applies here, as Tony uses that little 20 gauge almost exclusively for his shotgunning. He shoots it well, and knows its capabilities. Tony and I hunted Osceolas on the Seminole Reservation in the Florida Everglades a few years ago, and I chuckled when I saw Tony's guide looking askance at his choice of firearm. He was all smiles a few hours later, though, as he and Tony emerged from the bush with a fine gobbler. Though Tony is far from the only turkey hunter to regularly fill his turkey tags with a 20 bore, the guide's concern that it would make his job tougher was not unfounded. The added challenge imposed by the 20's limited range is a handicap most hunters choose not to accept, and few hunters would argue that it is the optimum turkey gun.

The big 10 gauge has its proponents. All else being equal, the 10 gauge can reach out a little farther than the 12. The question is whether or not the extra range (which is not that much greater than that of a 12 gauge chambered with three- or three-and-one-half-inch magnum shells) is worth the extra weight and recoil. For a few, the answer is clearly yes. For the majority of hunters, the answer is no.

The 12 gauge is far and away the most popular medicine for serious turkey hunters, for several reasons. Those chambered for 3 1/2", and even 3" shells approach the performance of a 10 bore, but are significantly lighter. Even 2 1/2" shells are available in magnum. The venerable green Remington Express shells in that length and #6 shot are deadly out to 40 yards in my old Ithaca Model 37. Shotgun manufacturers offer a variety of guns designed specifically for turkey hunting, and all the major shotshell makers offer 12 gauge shells designed specifically for turkey hunting. All these options allow hunters to select the combination of range, recoil, and price that they want, and to own a shotgun that is effective for game from quail and dove to waterfowl and turkeys.

How important is camouflage on a shotgun? If the finish is not shiny, blued barrels and brown or black stocks probably blend in well enough with most environments. Certainly thousands of turkeys are bagged each season by hunters carrying uncamouflaged shotguns. It is true, though, that the gun is the one thing that must usually be moved as a turkey approaches. Full camo surely can't hurt, and could conceivably make a difference in some situations. I haven't made up my mind on this one. I often use camo guns, or put a camo gun sock on my shotguns. At the same time, I have a handsome double-bore Pedersoli smokepole that I never cover in camo, and I've taken quite a few birds with it. (Be careful with camo tape, by the way--I have seen taped guns rust in a matter of hours in damp conditions.)

Pump, autoloader, single or double bore? "Pump over autoloader," insist some hunters, "because they're more reliable." Maybe so, and I'd buy that argument if the quarry were Cape buffalo or lion, but it's not. A good, well-cared-for autoloader is more than sufficiently reliable for turkey hunting. Properly done, turkey hunting is a one-shot endeavor anyway, except for the rare circumstance, so even a jam or a failure to chamber another round should not result in a lost opportunity. I normally hunt with a pump, by the way, but the reason has nothing to do with reliability.

"Autoloaders over pumps," insist some hunters, "because they reduce recoil." They've got a point. If recoil is a real concern for you, autoloaders may be the way to go. Not all hunters are bothered by recoil, and even those who are might reasonably point out that, once the gun is patterned, shooting those shoulder-punishing magnum turkey loads through it is a relatively infrequent occurrence.

Regardless of the kind of shotgun you prefer, one way to substantially reduce recoil is porting. Barrels can be ported for a reasonable cost, and ported choke tubes are widely available. There is some debate about whether or not the ported choke tubes are as effective in reducing recoil as ported barrels are, for technical reasons we needn't get into here. Either ported barrels or ported choke tubes do provide some reduction in recoil, though, and are worth considering, especially if you prefer light, short-barreled guns and insist on the maximum range offered by extra-full chokes and magnum shotshells.

I can see few arguments in favor of the single-bore shotgun other than light weight, economy, and safety for the young hunter. The double bore offers the second shot capability, but so does every other option except the single bore, and often at less weight. My friend Tom Cross, outdoor writer, veteran turkey hunter, and the fellow who helped me along when I was new to the sport, makes a good case for the double bore. Tom points out that of all the options, only the double barrel gives a hunter an instant selection between two choke sizes and two shot sizes. If a gobbler hangs up at forty yards Tom uses one barrel; if it sneaks in from behind and is slipping past at ten steps, he uses the other barrel. Further, as Tom points out, the double bore tends naturally to be shorter because the receiver is smaller than that on pumps and autoloaders.

Certainly there is nothing wrong with the single bore, and it may very well be the ideal gun for the youngster. And as Tom Cross points out, the side-by-side or O/U offers some unique advantages. The hunter who owns a double bore for waterfowling or upland gunning, and who decides to take up turkey hunting, can certainly be well-served in the turkey woods by his favorite double. Still, the battle between the traditional double barrel and the pump gun or autoloader was fought a long time ago, and in this country at least the pumps and the autoloaders emerged the clear victors in popularity.

Should the ideal turkey gun have a sling? I suspect most turkey hunters would say yes. Slings leave the hands free for hiking into and out of the woods, or for climbing steep hills, and they can be used as a sort of brace to steady the aim, in much the way rifle slings are used. I normally don't use a sling, even when the rifle or shotgun I'm hunting with is equipped with one. Over the thirty-plus years I've spent carrying rifles and shotguns afield, I can recall several instances in which I bagged game while entering or leaving a hunting area while my companion, with gun slung over his shoulder could only watch. Do several such instances over the course of a lifetime outweigh the convenience of using a sling? That's a personal call, of course, but for many serious hunters the answer is no. Since having a sling

109

doesn't require using it, I'll go with the consensus on this one and concede that the optimum turkey gun should be equipped with a sling.

Most turkey hunters will agree that the ideal turkey gun should be tightly choked to achieve maximum pattern density and longer range. Bring up the subject of maximum range for turkey guns at a hunting camp and sooner or later some (presumably) true turkey hunter is sure to point out that the true turkey hunter enjoys the challenge of calling birds in close. The implication, of course, is that real turkey hunters aren't overly concerned with extending the range of their shotguns.

There is some truth in that, and many turkey hunters at some point take up bow or muzzleloader for the added challenge, a challenge resulting in part from reduced range. Thousands of other hunters shoot open-choked or small bore guns, and are perfectly content to limit their shots to the effective ranges of those guns.

On the other hand, part of the challenge of any form of hunting is obtaining maximum performance from the weapon of choice, be it bow, muzzleloader, or shotgun. Heading out to the range to experiment with chokes, loads, and various shot sizes in search of the maximum effective range is part of the fun. I've spent countless hours seeking an elusive additional five yards from my favorite smokepole, when I could easily gain an additional ten yards by pulling my old Ithaca or Mossberg from my cabinet. For that matter, I have at least one other muzzleloader that would increase my range by the same margin. I enjoy experimenting with chokes, powders, wads, shot charges, or shotshells, trying to get the most from my guns.

How important is it that shotguns be chambered for three-and-a-half-inch shells? There is no guarantee that a three-and-a-half-inch shell will produce the best pattern in a given gun, nor is there a guarantee that magnum shells will perform better than their standard counterparts. My old Ithaca Model 37 is chambered for two-and-a-half-inch shells. The venerable green Remington Express outperforms every shotshell I've experimented with in that gun, including the two-and-a-half-inch magnums. The non-magnum load in that gun will kill turkeys cleanly out to forty yards. And there is no denying that those big three-and-a-half-inch shells are punishing. On the other hand, they do add pellets to the count, which can make for denser patterns downrange. They are very popular with a lot of serious turkey hunters. Since guns chambered for the long shells can also handle shorter ones, it's hard to find a downside to guns chambered for them.

Granted, if current trends continue shotgunners may one day be able to take turkeys at ranges that greatly reduce the challenge of the sport and substantially increase the harvest of turkeys. In that case, we might want to take a look at regulating the kinds of loads or guns with which hunters are allowed to pursue wild turkeys. In the meantime, we can head out to the range with patterning boards and targets and shotguns and ammunition and various other paraphernalia and have a lot of fun shooting.

What about sights? Optics, including scopes, red dot, and holographic sights are becoming increasingly popular among turkey hunters, but are still not nearly as popular as open sights. There are undeniable advantages to scopes, especially for hunters whose vision is less than perfect. Expense may be one factor in the continued preference for open sights, but there is certainly something to be said for simplicity. There is little to go wrong with open sights.

Given that turkey hunting requires precise shooting (compared to wing-shooting), the standard single bead sight is inadequate for turkey hunting. Two beads are better, but open rifle-style sights with fiber-optic beads have become the standard for most turkey guns. Our 'optimum' turkey gun, then -- if we accept the preceding arguments -- would be a short-barreled 12-gauge pump or autoloader chambered for three-and-one-half-inch shells, with an extra-full choke tube, in camo finish, with a sling and either fiber-optic sights or a low-power scope, red dot, or holographic sight.

If your passion for turkey hunting compels you to run out and buy the optimum turkey gun, I fully understand. Wild turkeys not only challenge hunters, they embarrass us on a regular basis. The desire to gain every legal and ethical advantage can be strong. And there is something to be said for pride of ownership, for the sense of pleasure to be derived from owning the best, and for hunting with confidence. Still, 'optimum' is a slippery term, and not to be confused with 'favorite.' My own current favorite turkey gun is my double-bore 10-gauge smokepole. It's too long, it's too heavy, and it does not have the range of a modern shellshucker. Why do I prefer it? Well, I like the way it looks. I like the heft of it, and the way it feels in my hands. I like the sense of tradition I feel when I carry it in the woods, the feeling of connecting with some unknown ancestor who once carried a similar fowling piece afield in search of game, quite possibly on the same hill I'm hunting. I like to hear the shot boom out through the valley and see the gray smoke roll when I let down the hammer. And I never do that without envisioning that other fellow, perhaps a century and a half ago, dropping the hammer on a turkey and waiting for the smoke to clear to confirm that his shot was true and his family will eat turkey for dinner. If I don't grab the smokepole, I usually reach for my old Ithaca Model 37, for no other reason than that I'm comfortable with it. I killed my first turkey with it many years ago, and I remember that event every time I pull that gun from the cabinet. In the final analysis being familiar with a gun, having confidence in it, shooting it well, and knowing its maximum effective range, is more important than a few extra yards of range, a few inches in barrel length, or the latest high-tech sight or camo pattern. Still . . . I have to admit I've noticed the ads for a certain short-barreled 12-gauge pump chambered for three-and-one-half-inch shells, with a sling, the latest camo pattern, fiber-optic sights, and a maximum range at least ten yards beyond anything I'm currently shooting. Should it catch my eye in a weak moment, I just might have to add it to my collection.

THE SHOT SIZE DEBATE

Disagreements over shotguns tend to be friendly in nature, while for some reason disagreements over the best shot size for turkey hunting can practically lead to fisticuffs. It's just one of those things turkey hunters tend to have strong opinions about. Everyone who has spent some time experimenting with patterning shotguns can agree on one point: There is no predicting pattern density or uniformity based strictly on shot size. A gun may produce a more effective pattern with No. 4 shot than with No. 6, though the shell with No. 6s contains hundreds of pellets more than the one with No 4s.

Though Nos. 4, 5, and 6 are far and away the most popular shot sizes among turkey hunters, Nos. 2 and 7 1/2 have their proponents. I know several turkey hunters who rely on No. 2 shot in states where it is legal, aiming at the wing butt instead of making head shots. I'm skeptical that this is the most effective approach, but can't speak from personal experience, never having tried it. As for 7 1/2s, biologist, writer, and life-long turkey hunter Lovett Williams has dispatched more than a few gobblers with that shot size.

For some this is a safety issue. According to insurance industry statistics, hunting in general is safer than swimming, soccer, baseball, bowling, and even pocket billiards. Still, though turkey hunting accidents seem to be declining nationwide, there is no denying that turkey hunting accounts for more than its share of accidents. The larger and heavier the shot, the greater the range at which it presents a hazard, and the more damage it can do at close range. Some hunters argue in favor of lighter shot for this reason.

My own preference is for No. 5s, which strike me as a good compromise between additional pellets for pattern density, and good downrange energy for penetration. However, I only use No. 5s when it patterns as well as, or better than, No. 4s or 6s. Between those three sizes, I'll use whichever size patterns best in a given gun.

There is a lot of talk in the shotshell industry about downrange energy. Some charts have been developed indicating that No. 6 shot cannot be relied upon to penetrate adequately at ranges beyond thirty-five yards. I applaud the inclination to be conservative about range, but I have to say I have bowled several turkeys over with No. 6 shot at ranges out to forty yards and slightly beyond, knocking them off their feet and killing them cleanly. There is an old saying among shotgunners that pattern density will become a problem before downrange energy does. Thus far I have let pattern density determine range for me, and I have yet to lose a turkey as a result of inadequate penetration. That is not to suggest that energy downrange is not a concern. Shotgun pellets shed energy rapidly, and smaller, lighter pellets shed them faster than heavier pellets. If you have a pattern that remains adequately dense at very long ranges, you should give some thought to this, particularly if you are using No. 6 shot or smaller.

Energy is something to keep in mind when considering magnum shells. In the past, magnum shotshells lacked the velocity of comparable non-magnum shells, because they contain proportionately more shot than powder. Manufacturers in recent years have addressed this discrepancy by producing high-velocity magnums.

A related aspect of shot selection is not size but hardness of shot. Shot may be deformed as it travels down the barrel and through the choke. The fewer deformed shot, the better the pattern. All else being equal, hard lead shot performs better than softer lead shot. Simply switching to copper- or nickel-coated shot can significantly improve a pattern. In addition to patterning better, hard, round shot penetrates better than soft or deformed shot.

CHOKES, EXTENDED FORCING CONES, BACKBORING

Shot charges flow through a barrel like water through a hose. The choke is often compared to the nozzle on a hose, constricting the shot charge into a smaller pattern. A key difference is that the results are far less predictable in the case of shot. There is a point, varying from one gun or shotshell to another, at which additional choke ruins a pattern.

Two points hold true about tightening shot patterns, though. First, it is the degree of choke relative to the bore size that determines pattern, as opposed to any absolute size. That is why a full-choke 20 gauge does not necessarily pattern tighter than a full-choke 12 gauge, though the diameter of the choke is much smaller in the case of the 20 gauge.

Second, all else being equal, shot that is more gradually constricted patterns better than shot that is constricted abruptly.

This explains why the modern, super-full-choke tubes extend beyond the barrel. It also explains the increasing popularity of lengthened forcing cones, a highly touted feature on many new shotguns. The forcing cone is the transition from the chamber to the bore-traditionally about three-eighths-inch long. Extending the forcing cone to at least two and one half inches can produce better patterns and somewhat reduce felt recoil. It is doubtful that extending the forcing cone beyond that length achieves any real benefits.

Back-bored barrels have become more popular in recent years as well. Simply put, a back-bored barrel is one that has been enlarged from the chamber forward to the choke. This can benefit patterns in two ways: First, a bigger diameter barrel means less deformed shot. Second back-boring makes the choke smaller relative to the bore, in effect increasing the choke. In fact, barrels that have had the choke removed can in effect have it restored by back-boring.

All these features-lengthened forcing cones, back-boring, and the installation of choke tubes-can be performed by gunsmiths on most modern guns and some older ones. Are they worth it? For the competitive sporting clays shooter looking for every edge, these are all important features. For the turkey hunter? That depends. The installation of choke tubes, if your gun doesn't already feature them, will make it more versatile, and will in all likelihood result in tighter patterns (probably much tighter patterns) with extended, extra-full tubes. The improvements offered by lengthened forcing cones and back-boring will usually be less dramatic. The cost for both would be less than the cost of a new pump shotgun. How badly do you want a slightly better pattern and slightly less recoil? How badly do you want a new pump shotgun that might already feature these options and would probably be shorter and lighter, handle three-and-a-half-inch magnum shotshells, and come decked out in the latest camo pattern?

"A turkey is a turkey."
                                         --Tony Knight, 1997

Chapter 13

HUNTING THE SLAM

Getting a slam is not really about claiming all the different subspecies of turkeys any more than turkey hunting is all about killing a turkey. It's about the opportunity to hunt turkeys in habitats ranging from forests, to mountains, to prairies, to swamps, and to near-deserts. It's about the travel getting to those places, and about the people you meet when you get there. It's about living with a sense of adventure, setting goals, and having dreams - important things that too many of us leave behind with our youth.

Hunting the slam is about travel, people, and hunting unique environments with different strategies. Swamp buggies are the only means of transportation in some parts of Florida.

A Grand Slam, just for review, entails taking the four subspecies of turkeys legal in the United States. A Royal Slam is those four plus the Mexican Goulds, and the World Slam is all those plus a separate Central American species of turkey, the Ocellated turkey. Some hunters think that a Grand Slam must be accomplished within one season, but I don't believe that's correct, and don't know where the idea originated. The first hunting slam of any kind that I am aware of was the Grand Slam on the various subspecies of North American sheep, and I am reasonably sure that taking all of them in one season was not part of the requirement. Slams of various kinds have become fashionable since then. (My friend Hank Strong, who loves hunting wild boar with blackpowder rifles, is trying to promote a Ham Slam, but he hasn't yet decided what it will consist of.)

It was on a south Florida hunt for Osceolas that I overheard Tony Knight of Modern Muzzleloading say, "A turkey is a turkey." Tony was responding to a question about what special tactics he planned to use in hunting Osceolas. Tony has a point, too. A turkey is indeed a turkey. All are extremely wary, all have excellent eyesight and keen hearing, and all of them have reflexes quick enough to easily snatch an insect out of the air. If they were any quicker, they'd duck under our shot patterns. That is not to say that hunters won't notice differences between the various subspecies. I suspect, though, that those differences have more to do with the amount of hunting pressure to which the turkeys are subjected, and to the varying environs they inhabit. Many hunters believe the western subspecies, particularly Rio Grandes, are less challenging than Eastern wild turkeys or Osceolas.

Not long ago I hunted a start-up operation run by David Mann near Bracketville, Texas. This is extremely arid country, dry and rocky, with cactus and mesquite comprising the bulk of vegetation. A few thin hackberries occupy the arroyos, and a rare live oak or two survives wherever conditions allow. My hunting partner on the trip, an experienced turkey hunter more familiar with the big woods and farms of the Midwest than the deserts of the Southwest, instantly pronounced it uninhabitable and clearly devoid of turkeys. Mann has run a deer and exotics hunting operation on the ranch for years, and access is strictly controlled. The morning after our arrival my hunting partner and I had an opportunity to hunt a section of the ranch on which turkeys had never before been hunted. Within twenty minutes of first light I had called in a pair of Rios and bagged one. The ranch limit is two, and not wanting to end my hunt immediately, I opted to await the arrival of the pickup truck that would take me in for lunch, with plans to bowhunt subsequent to that. By lunchtime, I had watched five gobblers pass by within shotgun range. My partner, when we met for lunch, happily conceded that the ranch was not devoid of turkeys after all. He, too, had bagged a Rio early in the morning and he, too, could have taken more.

David usually rotates hunters in camp to various parts of the ranch, shuttling hunters out for morning and afternoon hunts. Under those circumstances it was very easy to compare the behavior of the turkeys. There was little doubt that after several morning and afternoon hunts in the same vicinities, the turkeys were different birds - less vocal in general, far less likely to charge in immediately in response

116

to a few hen yelps, and warier. Additional turkeys were taken, to be sure, but getting them was the kind of challenge most turkey hunters expect. Are Rio Grandes less challenging than Eastern birds? When they've been subjected to less hunting pressure, yes.

The habitat is also a factor here. It is easy to locate turkeys when they are restricted to roosting in a strip of cottonwoods that line a stream flowing through the prairie, as is the case in many western states. Indiana is not a western state, of course, but when examining harvest statistics for Eastern turkeys in Indiana a few years ago, I was baffled to see success rates were dramatically higher in a few west-central counties than in the rest of the state, even though restoration efforts were comparatively recent there and turkey populations had hardly saturated available habitat. The explanation turned out to be simple: the west-central counties were heavily farmed, consisting mostly of cropfields interspersed with small woodlots, the woodlots being joined by windbreaks and the trees bordering streams. No problem finding the turkeys here; take a quick glance around and walk to the nearest woodlot, and that's where they'll be roosting.

If they're not in the woods, they're not hard to locate in the fields with a pair of binoculars, and there is little doubt about where they're going when they want shade or shelter. By contrast, Indiana's more traditional turkey habitat consists of big woods in hill country. The birds are there in impressive numbers, but finding them and figuring out where they're going is a little more challenging. Adopting Tony Knight's attitude that a turkey is a turkey is probably a safe way to go, especially for easterners venturing west. It can be helpful, though, to be prepared for the different kinds of habitat and the different hunting methods those habitats can dictate.

Osceolas

We'll start with the South Florida strain of wild turkey, which many turkey hunters consider the most challenging of all. They are supposedly less vocal than their close cousins, the Eastern wild turkey. If so, I've been very fortunate. I can't detect a difference between them, other than the slight variations in size and coloration.

One thing that does make the Osceola a challenge is the fact that it is available in only one place - the Florida peninsula. (Birds in the panhandle region are Eastern or Eastern-Osceola hybrids.) Osceolas are holding their own in terms of numbers, but habitat is shrinking faster in Florida than just about anywhere else, and finding a good place to hunt them can be difficult. Most hunters would do well to reserve a hunt with a lodge or outfitter. Turkey hunting operations can be expensive in Florida, but for the out-of-state hunter time spent locating land on which to hunt is expensive, too, especially if a lack of familiarity with the area, bad information, or heavy hunting pressure brings him back repeatedly to complete the Osceola leg of the Grand Slam. Though they don't advertise it, some turkey hunting operations are willing to negotiate a do-it-yourself hunt in which hunters pay what amounts to a trespass fee to hunt, taking care of their own accommodations, housekeeping, and game preparation. It never hurts to ask.

Author with Guide Doug Smith of Florida's Big Cypress Hunting Adventures and a fine Osceola taken at a range of 4 steps.

There is some good public land hunting available in Florida, including areas hunted by quota, and a new Special Opportunity Hunts program that involves permits by drawing. These are quality hunts and well worth applying for. Interested hunters should contact the Florida Fish and Wildlife Commission at 850/488-4676, or log onto their website. A key word search will turn up several avenues to access the site, and is probably easier than entering the ridiculously long website address: www.floridaconservation.org.

Hunting Osceolas often means hunting swamps or swampy areas, and it also usually means hunting in very warm weather. Take plenty of water and insect repellent, dress for warm weather, and wear snake boots if you're worried about rattlers. If you're on a do-it-yourself hunt, and if you get a bird, the warm weather makes being able to get your turkey cooled down quickly a priority. Apart from that, the hunter who hunts Osceolas as if he were after Eastern gobblers will not likely encounter any surprises.

Where else but in Osceola country does a turkey hunter's competition include gators, bears, rattlesnakes, wild boar, and Florida panthers?

Rio Grandes

In addition to being generally less challenging to hunt than Eastern birds, Rios are often thought to be more vocal and to travel in bigger flocks. I'm inclined to think they are more vocal precisely because they do travel in bigger flocks, in addition to receiving less hunting pressure in many places. I'm not sure why they travel in bigger flocks, but this could be habitat related. If adequate food exists to support the numbers but the food, along with roosting space, shade, and shelter, is concentrated in smaller areas, it stands to reason turkey populations would be concentrated as well.

The overwhelming majority of Rio Grandes are in Texas, though huntable populations exist in parts of Oklahoma and Kansas, too. Public land is limited in Texas; unless a hunter is fortunate enough to have friends or relatives who own land in Texas, he will have to pay to hunt Rio Grandes there. On the plus side, there are a lot of options, ranging from first-class haciendas with all the amenities and fully guided hunting, to do-it-yourself hunts out of bunkhouses or even simple trespass fee arrangements. A little homework checking ads in Turkey Call or Turkey & Turkey Hunting magazine, among others, can put hunters onto exactly what they're looking for. Just be sure, no matter how slick the ads or how well-known the operation, to check several references.

Success rates are high in Texas, but Rio Grandes can be as elusive as any wild turkey if subjected to hunting pressure.

The environments inhabited by Rio Grandes vary somewhat, but in many cases the hunter accustomed to pursuing Eastern gobblers will need to adjust his tactics, if only a little. I recall vividly my first hunt for Rio Grandes. The first thing I remember is that the stars were still shining brightly when birds began gobbling from the roost. Amazed, I hit the button to illuminate my watch. I don't remember now what it said, but it doesn't matter; it was still hard dark, and a good half hour before I expected to hear any gobbling.

The next thing I recall is that I had no idea how close the nearest bird was. Sound carries differently in the flat, wide-open spaces, and I couldn't even make an educated guess about the distance. Then I decided it didn't really matter how far away that gobbler was, because standing there surrounded by cactus and mesquite as the stars faded and the eastern horizon grew pale, the bird would see me from 500 yards away. I scampered for a place to set up. What a frustration -- standing, I could see for miles; sitting, I couldn't see twenty yards past the cactus and mesquite. Sound does in fact carry farther in wide-open country, and gobblers seem inclined to respond to calling from greater distances. Setting up on birds can be difficult, and relocating harder still, because of the greater visibility. On the plus side, relocating seems to be required less often, partly because Rios travel farther, partly because of the lack of gullies, creeks, and similar obstacles in most parts of Texas.

Merriam's

Hunting Merriam's turkeys in some areas is similar to hunting Rios, and for the same reasons. The birds are more vocal and tend to travel in bigger groups. Sound carries farther, and increased visibility can make setting up on or relocating these birds difficult.

Unlike Rios, though, Merriam's often inhabit mountainous country, and hunting mountain Merriam's involves one important distinction: Merriam's travel. Actually, they migrate, moving for miles to different elevations depending on the weather. In some cases they seem to like following the snow line, staying just behind the melting snow, but a late-season cold snap can send them hurrying back to lower elevations. When hunting Merriam's, you might get the impression that there is not a turkey in the county - and you might be right. They might be miles away at a higher or lower elevation. Seeking information from locals is time well spent, but sometimes there is no getting around the need to cover a lot of ground. Find them in the Ponderosa Pine country, though, and you can hunt them much as you would Eastern gobblers. Eastern Montana, Wyoming, western South Dakota, and New Mexico are among the better places to chase Merriam's, though they inhabit at least fifteen western states.

Many hunters think the Merriam's is the most strikingly beautiful of all the wild turkeys.

Ponderosa Pines are classic Merriam's habitat, though these birds often occupy prairie environments as well.

Eastern Turkeys

Given that they inhabit every state east of the Mississippi, and a few west of it, this is the turkey most hunters are familiar with. Are they the toughest subspecies to hunt? My friend Tony Mandile, from Phoenix, enjoys telling the story of his first hunt for Eastern gobblers. Seems the sun had not yet cleared the horizon on his first day out when he bagged a big tom. He's taken a few others since then, and I don't think he's convinced Eastern gobblers are any tougher than the western birds he's pursued. I suspect most westerners coming to the East to hunt turkeys for the first time would find it easier to set up on gobblers, as well as to relocate on them, and would feel that they could often use terrain and foliage to move about with comparative freedom. On the other hand, our hypothetical westerner might also find it a little more difficult to locate gobblers on some days, would discover quickly that they typically travel in groups no bigger than two or three birds in spring, and often travel solo, and would find them, with some exceptions, less vocal and more call-shy.

Which states offer the best hunting for Eastern turkeys? I've hunted very little in the northeastern states, but based on the hunting I've done in the Midwest and the South, I'd say it's a very tough call. The birds are continuing to expand rapidly in many areas, and I've enjoyed excellent turkey hunting in almost every state except North Carolina and Louisiana - states that I have yet to hunt. Certainly

Alabama has to be near the top of the list, along with Missouri. Iowa offers great hunting, and don't overlook states such as South Dakota, where turkey numbers don't rival those of more southerly states, but where hunting pressure is comparatively light and success ratios top those of many better-known turkey producers.

Eastern gobblers are the most familiar strain to millions of turkey hunters. Hard hunted and often difficult to fool, Eastern turkeys don't take a back seat to any of the subspecies.

Just Do It

The biggest problems in achieving the Grand Slam for most hunters are not the challenges of hunting any one species of turkeys. The problems are the obstacles most of us face. Our time is limited, our finances are limited, and our knowledge of other hunting areas is limited.

This is a great time to be a turkey hunter, though, and not just because of the remarkable comeback of the wild turkey. The resources available to us today can go a long way to reduce any limitations we face.

Take time, for instance. A three-day turkey hunt is a week-long excursion if it means two days driving to the destination and two days driving back, but thanks to bargain-basement airfares, it is now sometimes less expensive to fly than to drive. Especially if you live near a major urban area, chances are you can buy round-trip tickets to a lot of destinations very cheaply if you plan in advance and watch for bargains. I live less than thirty minutes from the Greater Cincinnati Airport, one of the most expensive places to fly from in the country. By driving an hour and a half to fly out of Louisville or Indianapolis, though, I've purchased roundtrip tickets for many hunting excursions for less than $200, and several for less than $100. I have a travel website monitoring airfares for me and sending me email notices whenever fares to certain destinations go below an amount I've specified. It's a free service; you can do it too. Travelocity.com will e-mail users when prices for given destinations fall below designated amounts. Expedia.com and several others will send weekly updates of best prices for desired destinations.

You can leave for a hunt in the morning, be hunting two time zones away that afternoon, hunt the next two days and the following morning, then be home for dinner the fourth day. You're away only two full days, and have hunted the equivalent of three full days. In some cases you might be hunting with outfitters who routinely pick clients up at the airport. In other cases you'll need to rent a vehicle. You might find a hunting partner who prefers to drive because he has the time or wants to bring a truckload of gear, who will stop by the airport to pick you up at the other end.

Financial limitations are a reality for all but a few fortunate hunters. To some extent they are a matter of assigning priorities, though. A fishing buddy of mine shook his head in wonder when I told him what I spend on dues and other expenses at a local hunting club. It sounded extravagant to him. He reacted this way as we stood casting from the deck of his new glitter-flake bass boat outfitted with fish-locators, sonar-guided trolling motors, and an outboard engine generating speeds that had my cheeks flapping around my ears. What he spent on that boat, forgetting gas, insurance, and maintenance, would pay my hunting club dues for life several times over. His boat struck me as extravagant. Different priorities.

Hunters needn't be pampered in world-class hunting lodges to enjoy great hunting. And when it comes to turkey hunting, only the least experienced hunters benefit from fully guided hunts. The rest of us just want to be pointed in the right direction. Camping can be a great way to keep costs down, and good hunting is available on public land in many states. Instead of spending money, spend the time doing the research on where to go. This not only saves money, it addresses the knowledge limitation as well. Ads in hunting magazines are good place to start, but don't forget the Internet. In a few hours time (or less) hunters can use the net to garner all the information they need about where to go and when to go, season dates, license and permit requirements, local outfitters, and more.

Advances in communications and data storage have contributed to the trend of swapping hunts, too. Organizations such as the North American Hunting Club, as well as a number of hunting-oriented websites, provide places for hunters to propose and accept such trades. A hunter might offer lodging in his home, cabin, or hunting camp, along with access to a good hunting area and possibly his expertise or guiding services, in return for the same services from another hunter elsewhere.

How likely this is to work for you depends in part on where you live and what you have to offer. If you live in Montana, for instance, and can offer a private-land elk hunt, rest assured you'll find plenty of folks perfectly happy to let you hunt their land or their hunting lease for any kind of turkey you'd care to go after. Private-land elk hunts aside, don't sell your local hunting short. Pheasant hunting on CRP land in Nebraska might seem like no big deal to some Nebraskans, but a hunter in Florida who is tired of shooting released quail over his pointer might happily offer a hunt for Osceolas on his hunting lease in return for a place to stay and local information about good places to hunt pheasants in Nebraska.

The bottom line is that the turkey hunter willing to do a little research and invest some time can enjoy quality hunting for every subspecies of wild turkey in the United States. The best thing about it is that, given the proper attitude, your next adventure can begin right now.

Author with a fine Gould's gobbler. Taking the slam is all about people, places, and a sense of adventure. A Gould's hunt in Mexico's Sierra Madres is hard to beat on all three counts.

Camping can give hunters access to remote locations and less pressured birds.

"It is not the size of the wilderness that is important. It is the quality of the involvement with it that makes the difference."

--Tom Brown
from *Tom Brown's Field Guide to
Nature Observation and Tracking*, 1983

Chapter 14

LEASING AND MANAGING SMALL HUNTING PROPERTIES

The gobbler was so far away I held little hope for bringing him in. Moving toward him to close the distance was not an option, since he was off the property and I was near the boundary line. Still, he kept gobbling in response to my high-volume yelps, so I continued calling until there was no doubt he was headed my way. More than an hour later, I heard the bird walking in the leaves; I eased my gun into position in expectation of bringing this long-range duel to a satisfying conclusion.

When I heard a twig pop to my right and slightly behind me, I froze, guessing a second tom was sneaking in from that direction. Then I heard a rustling in the leaves, then another step, and in my peripheral vision appeared a man wearing blue jeans and a gray jersey. He stood on his toes peering in the direction of the gobbler, then resumed sneaking slowly toward him as if he thought he were going to walk up to him and shoot him. The gobbler, not surprisingly, had fallen silent, and I had no doubt he was halfway to the next county by now. When I said "Howdy" the fellow nearly jumped out of his skin, then turned around and began sneaking off in the direction from which he had come. So much for the pre-season scouting I had done. So much for rolling out of bed at 3:30 a.m. and driving for more than an hour to get to that spot. This wasn't the first time my morning's hunt had been ruined that way, and in that very spot. It was private property, and the owner was a very good friend who had given me exclusive permission to hunt the place several years before. But it was close to town and easily accessible from three roads, and no amount of sign posting would keep poachers out. In accordance with the owner's wishes, I had invited a number of trespassers to leave the place, politely at first, much less politely as time went on. Prior to hunting that property, I had hunted some paper company land that was open to the public. It offered great hunting for a couple of years, but as turkey hunting grew in popularity, I began encountering increasing numbers of other hunters, and eventually crossed it off my list of hunting spots. Now, I had had it. It was past time to do something I had been putting off for years.

In Defense of Hunting Leases

Hunters from the South, or from other regions where leasing hunting property is a long-standing tradition, may have difficulty understanding this, but in areas where this tradition does not exist, leasing hunting rights is controversial. Many hunters, this one included, have fond memories of the days when a knock on the door of a farmhouse and a polite request often resulted in permission to hunt. And hunters in more remote areas recall days when land was not posted and they felt at liberty to roam the hills and forests, all of which were owned by neighbors, friends, and relatives.

Now, for a variety of reasons, farmers rarely grant permission to hunt their properties, and the hills and forests are less remote and consist of smaller holdings and lots, most of them posted. Hunting land is getting harder to find, and there is a legitimate concern that the leasing of hunting properties is paving the way toward the day when hunting will be an activity available only to the wealthy few, as it has become in most of Europe and some other parts of the world.

The issue runs deeper than affordability, though. Fish and wildlife are part of our American heritage, a natural resource thought to belong to all of us. In some countries, a grouse or a deer belongs to the person on whose property it is standing at the moment. Not so in this country, where wildlife belongs to the state, or the public, no matter where it resides. The notion of paying to hunt, as opponents of hunting leases put it, is viewed as nothing less than an attack on that heritage. A sympathy for those attitudes made me reluctant to take the step of leasing hunting property. I still have those feelings, but my attitudes about leasing hunting rights have changed over the years, for several reasons.

First, there is the hard reality that quality land on which to hunt is growing scarce, and leasing seems to be the wave of the future. Refusing to participate may be a principled stand, but it won't change that reality. Second, it may be, as some have argued, that a trend toward leasing hunting rights is good for wildlife, good for farmers, and good for hunting. Leasing hunting rights, or so goes this theory, simply reflects the fact that wildlife has real value. To the extent that wildlife has value, and hunting creates income, wildlife habitat will be protected and even improved. And only by preserving quality hunting can we hope to hand down the tradition of hunting to another generation. Finally, I discovered that leasing hunting property is not necessarily the expensive proposition I assumed it to be. When I got home from the ill-fated outing I recounted earlier, I called a hunting buddy, and a few days later we ran a short, simple ad in two weekly rural newspapers. It read something like this:

> Two responsible hunters seek land to lease for hunting. Must be at least 200 acres and loaded with turkeys and deer.

My phone did not ring off the wall. We got three calls in response to that ad, but that was all we needed. We began leasing a hunting property for less money than the two of us were spending on cable television, and since that day I've always shared at least one hunting lease with one or more hunting buddies. We hunt private property on which we have exclusive hunting rights. We bring guests, in accordance with rules we've agreed upon ahead of time. While trespassing is impossible to eliminate, we've managed to make it a rare occurrence. We can leave tree stands and blinds on the property. We can plant crops, bush hog, and clear trails, and generally manage the property for hunting. We enjoy safe, affordable, quality hunting. You can do the same.

Locating and Leasing Hunting Property

How easy it is to find land to lease, and how much you will have to pay for it, will be determined largely by where you live. In some areas - Texas comes to mind, as well as much of the South - leasing hunting property is a well-established and common practice. Some hunting leases have been held by the same family for generations. In these areas, it's a landowner's market. Finding a suitable property may take some time, and though prices are usually affordable when split between a group of hunters, hunters can expect to pay full value.

On the plus side, because they are accustomed to income from leasing land for hunting, many landowners in these areas manage for wildlife. They plant crops, mow hayfields, pasture goats, sheep, or cattle, and even do controlled burns, all with one eye on game management. In some cases, they have bunkhouses or cabins that can be used by hunters.

On the other hand, though trends are changing, there are still many areas in which leasing hunting property is not a well-established practice. The last time I leased hunting property in south-central Ohio (a few years before this writing), I had to explain carefully to landowners exactly what I was proposing, in some cases reassuring farmers that they would be giving up none of their rights as property owners, and that I wanted only the right to hunt on the property and engage in a few specified activities related to hunting.

The whole idea was alien to them, and they were suspicious. In these areas, land is usually easy to find, and relatively inexpensive to lease. In the case of marginal farming land, owners are often very happy to find that the land can generate any income at all. I know of a few cases in which hunting rights have been granted in exchange for the payment of property taxes.

The first step in finding property is the most enjoyable. Sit down with your potential lease partners and decide exactly what you need in the way of hunting property, depending on what you hunt, where you live, and how many of you are involved in the lease. Be realistic, too, about how far you will want to drive to get your hunting area. You might decide, for instance, that you and one partner need a minimum of 200 acres, that it should contain healthy populations of turkeys, deer, and ruffed grouse, and that it should be no more than ninety minutes from your homes.

There are some additional factors to consider. Make a list, in writing. Anything you can determine over the phone will save you a lot of time and running around. For example, you'll want to know if the owner hunts. Most hunters have no desire to compete with the person who lives on the place and can hunt it as often as he cares to step out his back door. I've turned down several otherwise attractive opportunities for that reason.

You'll want to know about access. Is there a creek that can't be crossed whenever it rains, for instance? Are there areas that are off limits to hunting for any reason? Are there logging roads?

How serious a problem is poaching in the area? Do the neighbors hunt? Do the neighbors allow hunting?

Does the owner farm the place? If so, will any of his farming activities interfere significantly with hunting? Does the owner have equipment for mowing, bush hogging, or keeping trails or roads open?

Does the owner sell timber? This can be good or bad. Limited, controlled logging is probably good, but you don't want to arrive to hunt one day and find that a big patch of woods has been clear-cut, or that loggers are in your favorite area with chain saws buzzing on opening day.

How heavily has the place been hunted in the past, and to whom have hunting privileges been granted? If the owner has never posted the place and it has been perceived as open to anyone who cared to hunt it, it will be difficult to stop poaching. I've even had experiences in which local hunters (and I hesitate to call them that) so resented the loss of "their" hunting property that they tore down and shot up signs and vandalized property to express their displeasure.

Negotiating Terms

When hunting leases don't work out, it's usually because of a misunderstanding. You don't want to invest a great deal of time in finding lease property, and possibly in managing it, only to have a dispute that ends up in a cancellation of the lease or a legal battle. That's why it is important to spell everything out and make sure all parties are clear on what is expected of them.

Some or all of the following points may be subject to negotiation, and some may not apply to your situation, but they represent a good starting point.

First, I've learned to always carefully define exclusive hunting rights. "Exclusive" should be a simple concept to understand, but often it is not. Somehow there usually turns out to be a nephew who grew up hunting the place, or a next-door neighbor who has always hunted opening day of deer season on the property, and it's tough for the owner to say "no" to such people. Often they're forgotten about until after the lease is negotiated and hunting season rolls around. Better to resolve this issue up front.

It's important to carefully delineate any ancillary rights you may want, keeping in mind that unless the farmer is a hunter himself, he will not anticipate many of the things that you will assume you are entitled to do as part of a hunting lease. Scouting, for instance, especially in the off-season, might be something the landowner wouldn't anticipate. Make sure he understands that you may need to scout at various times of the year. (If access is denied during the summer or any other time, that should be reflected in the price of the lease.) If you're a deer hunter, you will probably want the right to hang tree stands and leave them in place, and to do a reasonable amount of pruning to clear shooting lanes. You may want the right to plant food crops, to keep roads open, or to bush hog. You may want the right to bring guests to hunt with you. If the property is not already well posted, you will want the right to post the property, and you should ask for cooperation in prosecuting poachers. If the owner balks on that, you might have reason to suspect that poaching will be a problem. These are among the major provisions. If the owner is friendly and amenable to them, you might want to try going a little further. You might want to ask, for instance, if you can store blinds, treestands, decoys, and similar items in his barn. You might want to ask for an agreement that he will not mow or bush hog until after the spring nesting season, so turkey nests will not be destroyed.

Negotiation works both ways, of course, and hunters should retain some flexibility. On one lease, for instance, I made an exception to the exclusivity rule. A retired game warden lived across the road on the back side of the property, and in return for the privilege of hunting the place several times each season, he kept an eye on the place, running off poachers and even assisting in their prosecution in the case of a few repeat offenders. When a hunting partner and I leased the place, we felt this was a good arrangement and opted to continue it.

Finally, of course, there is the money. Hunting properties may be leased for as little as $1 per acre, and as much as $10 per acre or more, in prime areas, but a figure somewhere between those is more common, again depending on the area. In settling on a figure, remember that hunters do in many cases have something to offer the landowner besides money.

Hunters can help control poaching, for one thing. Most hunters are ethical and law-abiding, of course, but unfortunately the ones most visible to rural landowners are the few who are not. Many landowners in rural areas would gladly allow two or three responsible hunters onto their property on a regular basis for a fee, if doing so will significantly decrease the presence of unknown, irresponsible poachers who may litter, endanger livestock, damage fences or other property, hunt too close to houses, and so on. This is especially true in the case of absentee owners, particularly those who keep a cabin on the premises for weekend or vacation use.

Some access improvement and wildlife management activities may be of benefit to owners, as well, including controlled burns, bush hogging, planting of crops, and clearing of logging roads and trails.

Monthly payments are probably ideal, though quarterly payments may be acceptable. Other arrangements may leave hunters out of luck if the landowner reneges on an agreement; the sums involved can be enough to hurt, but are seldom enough to justify the costs of a lawsuit.

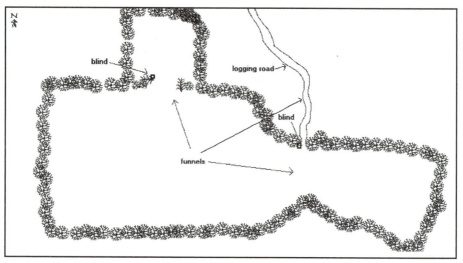

Meadow with Funnels. Chokepoint near east end at field is about 50 yards wide.

Any time and work spent managing the property is at risk if the lease expires in one year. It's probably best to negotiate a lease of three, four, or five years, specifying the right of first refusal when the lease is up. That won't guarantee that other hunters won't grab the lease out from under you, but at least it will give you the opportunity to match any bid.

In the end, you'll want to settle on a figure that all parties are comfortable with. Good will is worth a great deal.

Management

Wildlife biologists like to say that management activities are a waste of time on properties smaller than 10,000 acres, and some would say 20,000 acres. I have a great deal of respect for biologists, and on matters of science and natural history will usually accept their opinions over the frequently unscientific opinions of hunters.

Thing is, we're not talking science or natural history here, we're talking hunting. And when it comes to hunting, the smaller the property you're hunting, the more important it is that you manage it. Why? Chances are, if you're hunting 1000 acres of land in good turkey country, there are some good hunting spots on it - farmlands, bottomlands, hilltops, oak glades, meadows, and a diversity of foods and habitat.

If you hunt a seventy-acre patch of woods, the habitat is unlikely to be so diverse. Obviously, you want turkeys to have a reason to come to that area, and to spend a lot of time there. A woodlot that harbors only the occasional turkey passing through can be a turkey magnet if in the middle of that woodlot is a ten-acre pasture with a three-acre patch of chufa, winter wheat, or clover in it. Leave some good nesting cover around two sides of the pasture, clear a logging road through the middle of the tract, and you've got a hunting spot.

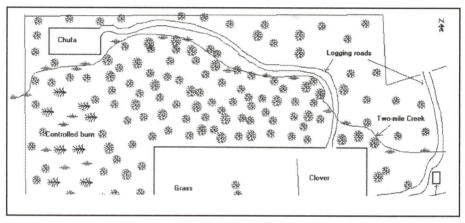

Small property managed for turkeys. Mixed habitat of woods, openings, logging road, and food plots will attract and hold turkeys.

I'm not suggesting that you lease a seventy-acre property; I'm just making a point. It may be true that boosting turkey reproduction in a small area is a spit in the ocean, but attracting turkeys to that area, and encouraging them to spend more time there, will improve your hunting.

Larger properties provide more in the way of management options for the ambitious hunter. First, determine what your property might be lacking in the way of turkey habitat. If it is mixed habitat consisting of some crops and some forest, including some mature trees, some second growth, some meadows or pasture, with a logging road or two cutting through it, it might be hard to improve on. A mixture of habitats that includes about twenty to thirty percent open land is probably ideal, though turkeys can do well on land that is fifty percent or more unforested.

Creating and maintaining openings on properties where these are lacking is probably the most effective turkey management tool. Openings can be pastures, meadows, cropfields, burnovers, logging roads, power-line easements - it doesn't really matter, so long as each opening covers at least an acre, preferably more. Some weed growth or brushy vegetation is also desirable. Turkeys rely on emerging green vegetation, grass seeds, and insects in spring and summer. At the same time, they are vulnerable in tall grass or thick growth. Hunters who are concerned about losses

133

to varmints probably could not find a better way to fight predation than to mow, bush hog, or use controlled burns to keep the understory thinned and the open spaces open. Cattle and sheep are probably the turkey hunter's biggest ally when it comes to improving turkey habitat, often making bush hogging and mowing unnecessary. And turkeys love to flip over cow patties to peck out the undigested grains and find the grubs and insects that live underneath.

Find a pasture away from houses, roads, or frequent intrusions, and you've probably found a turkey hotspot, assuming there are good numbers of turkeys in the area. Clover, winter wheat, chufa, and similar crops will attract and hold turkeys, not to mention deer and other game. Local farm supply or feed stores are good-sources of information about planting methods and times. Many state divisions of wildlife will provide seeds for food plots, either free or steeply discounted. Seeds are also available from the National Wild Turkey Federation, as well as from commercial producers.

Some hunters worry about water for turkeys, but water is a concern only in the most arid regions inhabited by turkeys, where water tanks or some other source may be helpful.

Controlled burns are useful, especially in areas dense with pines, and local agricultural extension agents or state wildlife managers will sometimes assist with these. Don't overdo it, though - a few small burns annually are better than infrequent bigger ones.

Managing properties for turkey hunting need not be a major undertaking. In many cases, farming operations already undertaken by the owner provide all the "management" needed to ensure good turkey hunting, and in other cases a sufficient diversity of habitat already exists to offer turkeys everything they need. Where additional efforts are required, the work need not be too time-consuming when shared by two or more partners. Leasing and managing hunting property can be, and usually is, a rewarding experience.

"When the creator made man and all the animals, they struggled for dominance.The turkey defeated a Seminole warrior and proudly stuck his scalp on itschest. That is how the turkey got its beard."

--Seminole legend

Chapter 15

THE TROPHY

Every mature gobbler is a trophy. I've yet to see a hunter who, no matter how many turkeys he has harvested in the past, did not spend a few moments admiring the gobbler he just killed. Most of us enjoy pulling out the tape to measure the beard and the spurs, even if we can see at a glance that they're on the small side. We smooth the feathers, noting the iridescence, and point out how the wing tips are worn from strutting, though we have seen that 100 times or more. We take turns hefting the bird by one leg and guessing its weight. No two gobblers are identical, but any real anomalies are quickly noticed - a missing spur, a kink in the beard, an odd coloration in the tail feathers, a scar. An Ohio gobbler I shot recently had pink spurs. He was a lone, dominant gobbler that a hunting partner and I had seen before and dubbed "Bad Boy," but in honor of those spurs we posthumously changed his name to "Liberace."

The best measures of a trophy are purely subjective. How memorable a given turkey is for me has far more to do with where I was hunting, who I was hunting with, and how much time I spent pursuing that gobbler than with how long its beard was. In considering the more standard, and most easily measured factors, most hunters agree that spurs are the best measure, since these are the best indicators of age in the field. Beards tend to break off, especially in northerly climes where they collect snow and ice balls. Body weight varies according to a number of factors. Corn-fed gobblers in farm country tend to be bigger than ridge-running turkeys in heavily forested areas. Northern turkeys tend to be bigger than Southern turkeys. (See sidebar for the NWTF trophy scoring procedure on page 74.)

As trophies go, there are a remarkable number of ways to display or make use of wild turkeys, from photographs to full body mounts, to displays of tails, beards, spurs, wings, capes, and feet. I routinely use wild turkey wing feathers in fletching my arrows, spending a fair amount of time making something I could buy inexpensively. Whenever I arrow a big-game animal or, for that matter, another turkey, I remember at some point the turkey whose feathers guided that arrow, and I get a kick out of knowing that bird has flown again.

In addition to those uses, I've donated feathers to Indian tribes who use them in religious ceremonies, and made wing-bone calls from the bones of my turkeys. Many of these possibilities are easy enough for any turkey hunter to do. Let's look at them in turn.

Photographing Your Trophy

A good photograph is probably the best trophy of all, because it puts the experience in a context, capturing forever the time, the place, and the people that were part of it. You do not have to be a professional photographer, or own expensive equipment, to get a great-looking photograph, if you just remember a few tips.

A good photo is the best trophy. Nothing else captures the time, the place, and the people along with the bird itself.

Start with good film. All but the cheapest cameras will take perfectly good photographs, but the same cannot be said about film. Don't scrimp here. Use trusted, well-known brands -- it's hard to go wrong with Fuji or Kodak. Avoid leaving good film in closed automobiles or other potentially hot places, and it will almost always perform as it should.

Carrying a small, point-and-shoot camera is a good idea. The sooner you get the photos the better. The bird will be in better shape. On a morning hunt, the light will probably be better earlier in the morning than at mid-day. Taking photos at the vehicle is next best. I've never been satisfied with photos taken at home. The two mistakes most often made by amateur photographers are 1) failing to fill the screen with the subject, and 2) failing to reduce contrast by using light properly.

Filling the screen is easy enough if we are conscious of the need to do it when we take the photograph. If we don't think about it, the subject looks close and we click away. Later, we're surprised at how small and far away things are in the photograph. Be objective about it, by looking through the viewfinder and determining that, for instance, the hunter's head almost touches the top of the viewing area, the turkey's head almost touches the bottom of the viewing area. (Some cameras are "what-you-see-is-what-you-get," some aren't, so take several slightly different shots to make sure you don't cut anything off.)

Film lacks the ability to "see" a wide range of contrast in lighting, which is why the face of a hunter wearing a cap comes out so dark as to be almost unrecognizable. If we compensate by admitting enough light to expose the shaded face properly, we get an over-exposed photo with washed-out colors. Shadows from trees, or anything else, tend to be harsh, looking like black bands across the picture. There is little we can do to control natural light, but we can take a few steps to reduce this problem.

First, avoid setting up so that part of the photo is in shade, part is in sunlight. This is an impossible situation. Get the photographer and the subjects in the same light, with the sun over the photographer's shoulder. Pull caps up, turn them around, or take them off, to get shade off the faces. Keep shadows out of the picture as much as possible. If your camera has a flash, take at least some photos with the flash, but remember that the small pop-up flashes on most cameras have a very limited range, sometimes as short as a few feet.

The hunters, and not the trophy, are truly the subjects, but it's important to display the turkey well, too. Wipe off any blood that may be obvious. Spread the wings out, to show off the size of the bird and make it appear more natural. Many hunters want the beard to show, and that is easy enough to arrange. A bird with a fanned out tail is the classic turkey hunting hero shot. If the turkey is held by a standing hunter, it should be held by the legs, and never by the neck.

Finally, cover yourself the same way the pros do - take lots of photos. Take photos with a vertical, and with a horizontal orientation. Get closer, get farther away. Use the flash and don't. Change exposure settings and speed, if possible, and try several different locations. Chances are you worked hard and invested a lot of time to get here, and this is a memorable moment. Don't be stingy with film.

Displaying the Tail, Wings, Beards, and Spurs

At the risk of offending taxidermists, you can do a better job on a turkey tail display than most taxidermists can. The methods most of them use make turkey tails look smaller, duller, and less natural than the display you can make yourself, very easily and at virtually no cost.

You can easily make your own tail and beard displays.

Most of the home methods I've read about for making this display involve the purchase of various kits or the injection of preservatives. I will guess that there is a good reason for these measures, but I will say this: over the years I've followed the simple steps below, and still have on my wall a tail that has been there at least ten years. I have some extras that have been lying about in my basement workshop almost as long, and I've given several away to friends who have them on display in their homes. I've not yet experienced feathers falling out, infestations, or any other problems. Keep in mind, if you wish to make your own turkey tail display, that you have the option of taking it to a taxidermist at any point in the process if you encounter problems. So long as you've preserved the tail feathers and the main coverts in good shape, a taxidermist should be able to provide you with the same kind of display you'd have gotten had you taken it there to begin with.

To prepare a tail for display, start by making sure the feathers are clean and dry. Grasp the tail feathers in one hand and cut them off at the base, being sure to leave enough flesh so the main tail feathers, as well as the shorter coverts, cannot pull out separately. You can always trim excess flesh away, and will usually need to. After you do this, wipe off as much fat or excess oil as you can, then sprinkle liberally with Borax. (The 20-Mule Team variety will do. Salt is not a good substitute.)

It's important to fan the tail open and keep it in that position until it stiffens. This can be delayed for a few days or even longer if necessary, but the sooner you do it the easier, and once the tail stiffens in a closed position, it can be difficult or impossible to open. A piece of stiff cardboard is the easiest mounting board to work with, but plywood will do. Fan the tail open (I like to spread it all the way out so that the base is level; many taxidermists fan the tails in a "V" shape.), and carefully insert pushpins or nails into the board between the feathers, near the base of the tail, to keep the tail fanned. It is not necessary to put pins between all the feathers. Put the fanned-out tail in a relatively cool, dry place where varmints, pets, or flies cannot get to it. Air-conditioned rooms are ideal.

Basements are fine if they are not damp. You will want to take a look at the tail every few days, possibly trimming off additional flesh as it dries, wiping off any fluids, and liberally applying Borax, making sure it reaches and covers every bit of flesh remaining - which should be very little. After about three week s- maybe less- the tail may be removed from the board and put on any of the display plaques available from catalog companies that sell turkey-hunting gear.

Most hunters like to display the beards and spurs with the tails. Beards are very easy - simply grasp them firmly and cut them off at the base. Remember that you can always trim away excess flesh, but if you cut too short and the filaments begin falling out, the beard is ruined. After trimming away excess flesh and wiping it off, sprinkle it liberally with Borax and put it away with the tail. Check it occasionally for a few days, trimming off additional flesh if necessary and re-applying Borax. After it has thoroughly dried out, wrap the base with electrical tape.

Spurs require just a little more work. Cut off the legs and apply Borax at the cut to preserve them if you are not going to get to the spurs immediately. To remove the spurs, saw through the leg bones just above and below the spur. Use a pocketknife to scrape all the scales and flesh from the bone, and clean out the inside of the bone with a paper clip or pipe cleaner. Exercise a little caution here; the bones are brittle and will snap if too much pressure is applied. The spurs themselves consist of a horny covering over a base of bone, and it is possible to scrape this off if you're not careful.

Most hunters consider the spurs to be the best indicator of trophy status.

Wings can be spread to make attractive displays. I've found wing displays more difficult than tail displays, though I've tried only a few. It could be that I did not remove enough flesh from the wings, or did not apply Borax frequently enough or in sufficient quantity. In any case, my experience with wings leads me to suggest that you either turn to a taxidermist for this, or buy one of the commercial kits that may include formaldehyde or other powerful preservatives.

Turkey wings can be turned into attractive displays. Note differences between Osceola wing, at left of photo, and Eastern gobbler wing, at right.

I would make the same recommendation regarding whole turkey skins. Hunters with some taxidermy skills can probably do it themselves, but I have never tried it. Feet can be mounted and made into bookends or other displays. They can be bronzed, as well. Again, I'd recommend a taxidermist for this.

Whole turkey mounts are increasingly popular, and of course this is a job for a good taxidermist. Hunters can do a lot to ensure a quality mount, beginning with selecting the right bird to mount. Any adult gobbler is a worthy trophy, but a turkey that is badly shot up, or that is soaking wet from rain or from falling into a swamp or puddle, is probably not a good candidate for mounting. Assuming the turkey is in relatively good shape, immediately wipe any blood or other fluids off

141

the feathers with a damp cloth. Some experts recommend plugging the vent and the beak with cotton balls. I've never known this to be necessary unless the bird is bleeding or discharging fluids, in which case it is probably a good idea.

If the turkey is damp, it must be dried off. A hair dryer will accomplish this in minutes, or sprinkle corn meal on the bird and ruffle it through the feathers, repeating this process until the bird is completely dry.

Tuck the turkey's head under a wing and take it to a taxidermist as soon as possible, checking it occasionally to smooth feathers or wipe it off. Ideally, the bird will be boxed carefully to protect the tail feathers and to keep flies and vermin away. Putting the turkey in panty hose is a great way to protect it and keep the feathers smoothed, and I recommend it, especially if the need arises to freeze the bird, which you will have to do if you cannot get it immediately to a taxidermist.

Some Indian tribes, especially in the Southwest, regularly use turkey feathers in religious ceremonies. The feathers are consumed in the process, so there is a need for a steady supply. Many hunters enjoy donating their feathers for this. In recent years, these tribes solicited the donations in classified ads in the back of turkey hunting magazines, especially Turkey Call, the official publication of the National Wild Turkey Federation.

Wing-Bone Calls

The few hunters who make and use wingbone calls tend to have strongly held beliefs about the "right" way to make a wing-bone call, implying, for instance, that only the smaller radius of a hen wing bone inserted into the ulna of a gobbler wing bone will make the proper sound, or that the sweetest tones are to be elicited only from wing bones made from jakes, and so forth. Those debates are entertaining, and I hesitate to take the mystique out of a wonderful and effective call, but the tone of any wing bone will be influenced by how far the smaller bone is inserted into the larger, by trimming the large bone so the opening is not as big, or by similar methods, and in any case no two hunters are likely to elicit precisely the same sound from a given call. I once met a hunter who could get some pretty good yelps out of a soda straw.

Essentially, a wing-bone call is made from inserting a turkey wing bone into another wing bone that is big enough to accommodate it. Some calls use three, instead of two, bones. The bones come from between the second and third joints of the wings. The bones are removed, then boiled for fifteen or twenty minutes, and cleaned inside and out thoroughly with knives, steel wool, bottle brushes, or pipe cleaners.

They may be sawed off at the joints, or filed partway through and snapped apart. Then they're sanded and smoothed down. It is often easier to make the call if bones are available from different turkeys, ideally gobblers and jakes, or gobblers and hens. Then it is an easy matter to find bones that will fit easily into other bones. Most hunters like to soak the bones in a mixture of bleach and water to whiten them. The bones are inserted one inside another and glued with silicone rubber or other cements in such a way that all the space is filled, taking care not to plug up the inside of the call itself. Hunters dress them in various ways with rubber bottle stoppers as lip guides, penholders for keeping them in the pocket, lanyards, and so forth. Artistic types draw designs on them with ink, or even etch them.

The caller typically cups his hands over the end of the call, and sucks air to create yelps, clucks, and kee-kees. Making them is a chore, and they are among the more difficult calls to master, but there is an undeniable mystique about wing-bone calls, and they impress turkeys and turkey hunting buddies alike.

Wild Turkey Feather Fletching

Most bowhunters prefer those pastel plastic things on their arrows. In fact, plastic vanes do offer some real advantages, but there is something to be said for feathers, too, so I'll make a brief case for them: they're virtually weightless, so they boost arrow speed; they're more forgiving of contact with the arrow rest; and they offer better control of broadheads. If you use feather fletching, or want to give it a try, why not make your own fletching from wild turkey feathers, simply for the satisfaction of it?

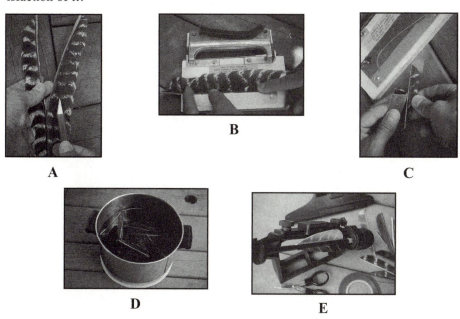

Making fletching from wild turkey feathers requires only a few simple tools.

A) **Split feather with sharp blade or razor.**
B) **Place on stop of feather chopper and chop out fletch.**
C) **Sand quill to smooth.**
D) **Die cock feathers.**
E) **Fletch arrows.**

143

If you already have the tools to fletch or repair your own arrows, chances are you have everything you need except a feather chopper or burner. I recommend the chopper, which you can buy from just about any place that sells traditional archery equipment. I've purchased two on-line. Order the size you want, and the shape. Most bowhunters prefer the modern, parabolic shape, but there are other options.

Remove the wing feathers from any turkey. Pruning shears will do this job quickly and easily, but remember that if you fletch with a right helical, only feathers from the right wing will work, and vice-versa. In most cases, count on getting one fletch per feather. Start by splitting the quill lengthwise with a sharp knife. An X-acto works great.

Place the feather on the chopper. (It will come with directions, but its proper use is almost self-evident.) Whack it a good one and get your fletch. The middle part of the feather, where the quill is neither too thick nor too thin, works best. Sand down the underside of the quill to smooth it. You'll quickly reach a point of diminishing returns, so don't aim for perfection. Getting a cock feather of a different color is easy to accomplish with Ritz die, available in most drug or grocery stores. Heat the die in a pan, drop the feathers in, making sure all are covered, then leave them until the die cools sufficiently to remove them.

Nothing left to do now but fletch your arrows as you would with store-bought fletching. That, and feel smug.

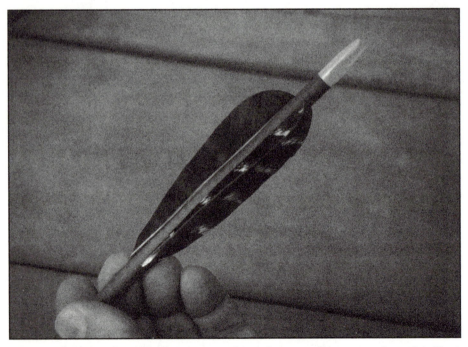

The finished product looks great and works as well as store-bought. Best of all, the turkey you killed last spring can fly again!

"In the woods we return to reason and faith."
--Ralph Waldo Emerson

Chapter 16

FALL TURKEY HUNTING

Fall turkey hunting is becoming increasingly popular as turkey populations expand and more and more states open fall seasons. Make no mistake about it, fall turkey hunting is a different sport. Fall hunters can use the same camo, the same guns (or bows), and the same calling devices. Hunting strategies, though, are usually very different, because in many ways fall turkeys are different creatures than spring birds.

Understanding Fall Turkeys

In the spring, turkeys are preoccupied with breeding. For spring gobblers, even eating takes second place to finding mates. Toward that end, both gobbler and hen flocks break up in late winter or early spring, with hens generally seeking solitude for breeding and nesting, while gobblers struggle to establish dominance and win breeding rights. Gobblers often travel in groups of two or three birds, sometimes more, but in each such group there is a dominant bird to whom the others are subordinate. The priorities of breeding season give rise to certain vulnerabilities. Gobblers may move toward hen calls, in hopes of mating, and may move toward gobbles or other sounds made by gobblers, which they perceive as challenges to their dominance.

In the fall, survival and eating are the only objectives. Birds are typically in flocks consisting of hens with their offspring from the previous spring, flocks of gobblers, and flocks of hens that did not successfully nest. At some point in the late fall or winter, the previous spring's male offspring, or jakes, form their own flocks. Fall is a time of plenty for turkeys. Berries are ripe and mast, especially in the form of acorns, is widely available. Turkeys spend a great deal of time scratching for acorns in the fall. Though fall ranges may overlap those of spring, they are not the same. Areas that held turkeys in the spring may be devoid of birds in the fall. Further, since turkeys are in flocks, they are not distributed as widely over a given area.

Turkeys do have some areas of vulnerability at this time of year. One of them is that in most states any turkey is fair game during the fall season, including hens and young of the year. Mother turkeys and last spring's poults are vulnerable because they tend to be noisy. They're not as noisy as a gobbler ringing through the woods, but hens and young turkeys in the fall do a lot of yelping, clucking, purring, and scratching, all of which can be heard for some distance by an alert hunter. Their other vulnerability is a strong tendency to stay with the flock. Separated, they become desperate to reunite, and they call loudly, often mixing the kee-kee-run, a high-pitched, whistling sort of call characteristic of young turkeys, with yelps, clucks, and other vocalizations. Further, these young of the year are inexperienced and are much less wary than adult birds.

You might believe that this makes fall turkey hunting less challenging than spring turkey hunting, and most experienced hunters would agree with that assessment, with one exception: fall gobblers. Gobbler flocks tend to be comparatively loose aggregations of birds. The adult gobbler seems to enjoy male companionship, but he's not desperate for it. If gobblers become separated in the fall, they'll usually get back together, but in their own good time. "Their own good time" is usually a matter of hours, but may be a matter of days. They will move through the woods clucking on occasion, and might even yelp now and then, but will refrain from the kind of loud and frequent vocalizations characteristic of young turkeys reuniting or hens calling out to their youngsters.

Many experienced turkey hunters considering taking a mature fall gobbler as a supreme accomplishment.

146

For this reason, many experienced hunters consider killing a fall gobbler to be a greater challenge than killing a gobbler in the spring. In fact, to many of our grandfathers who hunted turkeys in those areas where the turkey hunting tradition never died out, hunting spring gobblers was considered unsporting. Slipping up on gobbling toms and calling them in with hen calls seemed like cheating to many old-timers; for them, turkey hunting was strictly a fall affair.

Fall Hunting Strategies

Based on the above, two things should be clear: Fall hunting strategies will generally differ greatly from spring strategies, and fall strategies will differ depending upon whether the quarry is family flocks or gobblers. The commonly accepted strategy for hunting family flocks entails locating a flock and flushing it in a way that will cause maximum separation, then setting up and calling to bring the flock, or at least one member of it, to the caller. It is easy to determine whether a flock is using a given area, since there will be fresh scratchings all over the place. A few turkeys moving through the woods will leave telltale evidence behind, and the scratchings of a big flock moving through an oak glade are unmistakable, and are visible from long distances in the open woods.

Flocks are occasionally sighted, but usually the hunter locates flocks by slipping quietly through the forest and listening intently. A flock of turkeys scratching in the autumn leaves makes quite a ruckus; a roosted flock, both evenings and mornings, will usually be quite vocal. The ideal fall hunt begins, in the opinion of many, when birds are roosted in the evening. The hunter then marks the spot and waits until dark, when the birds are settled in on the roost. Then he slips in close and runs through the center of the roosting area shouting, whistling, beating trees with sticks, attempting to flush the birds in different directions. The turkeys won't try to get together during the night, but will find new roosts. First thing in the morning they'll try to regroup at or close to the area of their original roost. The hunter will be waiting for them in that spot at first light.

Locating a roosted flock in the early morning is the next best scenario. Again, the hunter will slip in as closely as he can without being detected, then rush the flock, making a lot commotion and flushing the birds as widely as possible.

The hunter who has not roosted birds will attempt to locate a feeding flock during the day. He'll try using hills or other cover to get close, or he might determine their direction of travel and loop around to wait for them. Either way, he'll rush into the flock to scatter it, then set up to call. A family flock will begin calling to one another within twenty minutes, usually less.

The key in any of these scenarios is to scatter the birds widely. If they fly in the same direction, they'll regroup and the hunter will have little chance of calling them in. Often a group of young birds won't flush far, and it's possible for the hunter to follow up quickly and break these groups up into smaller groups, which is always a good idea when possible.

Hunters should be alert to the yelping of the hen in a family flock.

Sometimes hunters can yelp to bring in fall birds, but they cannot compete with the mother hen, as the youngsters know her voice. It's important to bring the youngsters in quickly, before Ma rounds them up. If possible, hunters should run the hen off. (Most hunters refrain from shooting the hen out of a family flock, though a lone hen or a hen in a flock of hens without youngsters is fair game.) Some hunters worry that the commotion involved in running off the hen will spook young turkeys, and indeed it might. On the other hand, the youngsters will key in on the hen's yelps and go straight to her anyway, so there is usually nothing to lose by getting her out of the picture if possible.

If ever it makes sense for two or more hunters to hunt turkeys together, fall hunting is that situation. Multiple hunters can sometimes effect a better flush than one hunter can, and in the case of desperate turkeys trying frantically to regroup, two or even three hunters in the picture does not increase the challenge the way it does in spring. In addition, it is often possible to shoot two or three birds, where legal, out of such a flock. Hunters who take one bird should simply stay put and continue calling for at least as long as they can hear turkeys kee-keeing in the area.

Hunting Fall Gobblers

Hunting fall gobblers is a real challenge since, as previously mentioned, they are not so desperate to regroup if separated. Nor are they often susceptible to hen calls. Turkeys are social creatures, and any turkey may respond to sounds made by another turkey, but with their brains unaddled by testosterone, gobblers are more cautious, and less likely to approach a hunter scratching out hen calls.

How to hunt birds without these vulnerabilities? It's tough, but fall gobblers do have a few chinks in their armor. Many hunters pursue them much the way they hunt family groups in the fall, attempting to break up flocks and call them back together. The difference is that in fall hunting, most hunters don't expect gobblers to begin trying to regroup for at least an hour or more. The key is having the patience to wait them out. Some hunters, upon breaking up a flock of fall gobblers in the morning, will leave the area and come back in the afternoon to begin calling. If the birds are flushed in the late afternoon, or off the roost in the evening, they will usually begin looking for one another the next morning.

As mentioned, fall gobblers tend to cluck to locate one another. In some cases they yelp quietly. Fall hunters do the same, listening carefully for clucks or gobbler yelps and occasionally making these calls themselves. It's important not to overdo it. Fall gobblers cluck only occasionally, and when they hear one another cluck, they usually drift gradually toward one another This is not usually the time or place for continuous clucking, long, emphatic yelping, cutting, or other types of aggressive calling, though occasionally scratching in the leaves can add some realism to your calling.

Contrary to popular opinion, gobblers do gobble in the fall. I've heard turkeys gobble every month of the year except July and August, and I'm sure I've not heard them then only because I spend little time in the woods in July and

August. They gobble much less in summer, fall, and winter, though.

Hunting fall gobblers like this is a real challenge, as the birds are not desperate to regroup if separated.

From a hunter's perspective, the use of a gobble in the fall is that it will sometimes elicit a response from a tom, enabling him to locate the birds. In addition to a comparatively weak inclination to seek the company of other gobblers, there is one other chink in the fall gobbler's armor, and that is that he can - to some degree - be patterned. Readers who live in rural areas are probably already aware of this, since they may observe a flock of turkeys in the same field day after day, or crossing a road in the same spot frequently These patterns aren't hard patterns; they're subject to the influences of weather or to disturbances by humans or predators, and they change, sometimes lasting only a few days, other times a few weeks.

In some woods that I've deer hunted regularly for years, but which is not open to fall turkey hunting, I've discovered an area where I can spot two or three gobblers traveling together almost every time I'm there, about 2:00 or 3:00 in the afternoon. Massive scratchings in the area, fresh ones and old ones, caused me to be alert in that area when walking to my stand for afternoon deer hunting, and soon I was spotting the gobblers regularly. They nearly always spot me first, and are moving away when I glimpse them through the trees, but my disturbances don't alarm them enough to keep them out of the area. Gobblers have been in this area in the afternoon for several years now - not every day, mind you, but more days than not. That area in south-central Ohio will be open to fall turkey hunting for the first time this year, and I know where and when I'll be hunting.

Short of visually patterning birds, hunters determined to bag a fall long-beard can simply hunt on the basis of sign - gobbler tracks and droppings, especially when they include old and fresh sign mixed together, indicate regular use, and hunters can set up in these spots and wait for the birds to show up, much as a deer hunter waits by a rub line or a food source and waits for a buck. Clucking occasionally is a good idea, since it might bring birds in, or at least cause them to reveal their presence by answering back.

As turkey populations expand and more states begin offering the option of fall turkey hunting, this variation of the sport will undoubtedly become more popular. Hunters who scout thoroughly and pursue gobblers with stealth and patience will eventually be rewarded with an autumn longbeard. Less particular hunters seeking any wild turkey to grace the Thanksgiving table will do well to hunt more aggressively, covering ground to locate flocks, then scattering the flocks and calling to bring in young birds. The debate about the relative merits of fall versus spring hunting may never be resolved, but one thing most hunters can agree on is that the plump, well-fed turkeys of autumn are superior even to spring turkeys on the table.

"Time is but the stream I go a-fishing in. I drink at it; but while I drink I see the sandy bottom and detect how shallow it is. Its thin current slidesaway, but eternity remains."

--Henry David Thoreau, *Walden*, 1854

Chapter 17

ZEN TURKEY HUNTING

Small wonder that many of us are all but blind and deaf; everything about our increasingly urban society conspires to dull the senses. We slide into an air-conditioned car in an attached garage and commute to an air-conditioned workplace. At day's end we return home in the air-conditioned car, pull into the garage, walk into the air-conditioned home, and complain about the heat.

We spend the work week looking at the world through glass, and for more than a few of us, the primary contact with nature is in the form of the carefully cultivated, meticulously landscaped pseudo-environment of a golf course. We spend the better part of our youth responding, like Pavlov's dogs, to school bells. As adults, we work ten-hour days and have a pager on our belt, a mobile phone in our car, and a fax machine in our home. Our days are an endless succession of meetings and phone calls, and always there is a report to be filed, a project to be completed, a deadline to be met.

Is it any great mystery that, in the unlikely event we should take up turkey hunting, we walk when we should sit, get tired and sit when we should be covering ground, call too early and abandon spots too quickly, fidget, slap bugs, complain that the turkeys are "henned up" or have been educated by pre-season callers, and leave the woods after two hours, having seen and heard nothing?

Okay, so my example is a extreme, and maybe even unfair. If at least part of that diatribe doesn't apply to you, though, you're part of a rapidly shrinking minority. Most of us are to some degree a product of an environment that's not too different from the one described--an environment that distances us from nature, conditions us to measure success in numbers, and programs us to expect results ASAP.

151

Can an impatient person learn to hunt turkeys effectively? The answer is yes--but he will have to cultivate a good many strengths to overcome that handicap, and it will always be a handicap.

Slow Down

If you have ever enjoyed an extended stay in the wilderness, you almost certainly found yourself slowing down, adjusting to natural rhythms, and becoming more fully aware of your surroundings. Given a lifetime of conditioning, though, and given that contact with nature is for most modern hunters limited to day trips and occasional brief forays into areas that are less than remote, learning to really see, hear, and understand the natural world requires not just time afield, but a conscious effort to change the way we experience nature.

One of the best deer hunters I know prefers to still-hunt. He follows the same regimen almost every time he hunts. He leaves his vehicle, walks 200 yards into the woods, sits against a tree, and closes his eyes. For ten minutes or so he doesn't move; then he stands slowly and begins hunting. It is his way of leaving the modern world behind. When he starts seriously hunting, he is not thinking about time. If he has a specific objective toward which he is heading, he does not allow himself to think about when he will get there.

Understand that this is not an either/or, on/off quality, but a state of mind that can be achieved to varying degrees, and which improves with practice. To some extent, it's simply a matter of being tuned in to the surroundings. As a lifelong hunter, when I drive down a country road with my family, I am aware of a constant parade of sparrow hawks on the phone wires, squirrels on fenceposts, deer in meadows, woodchucks and turtles on the roadside, and so on. I don't mention most of them, partly because my family would quickly tire of my running narrative, and partly because they won't see most of those creatures even when they're pointed out.

On the other hand, I've never achieved that level of awareness to the degree that my father did. Even in his later years, as his vision deteriorated, he invariably spotted deer or other wildlife before I did--proof to me that, while visual acuity is an advantage, knowing where to look and how to look at it is even more important.

How does one achieve this heightened awareness of surroundings? Again, though practice and experience help, they are inadequate in themselves. Explaining such an abstract and subjective process is difficult, but over the years I have gleaned the following tips from world-class trackers, hunters, and wildlife photographers.

Seeing and Hearing

To begin with, most of us develop a tendency to see and hear only what is close and directly in front of us. Not surprising, considering that we spend most of our time in boxes. On top of that, we're programmed to get from Point A to Point B, which means we don't pay a lot of attention to anything along the route. We watch the ground immediately in front of us to avoid stumbling over things, and shut out all else. There are times when the hunter needs to cover ground, move quickly, or even run; more often the hunter should move at the pace of a sloth, or sit or stand motionless. Either way, though, the idea is to engage all the senses and to use peripheral vision to remain aware of what is going on everywhere within the visual field. This is the way most of the animals we hunt see, including turkeys. It is probably the way humans were meant to see, as well, but if so it is a habit most of us have lost.

Regaining it requires refraining from focusing on individual spots. The overall vision is not as sharp, but the viewer is more sensitive to motion over a much larger area. When motion is detected, the vision is then directed to the source. With effort and practice, it becomes habitual and increasingly effective. Improved hearing is more easily achieved. We are all in the habit of tuning out a lot of irrelevant noise. In the woods, there is very little noise. Nearly every sound is conveying potentially useful information; we just have to remind ourselves of this until we stop tuning out sounds and instead pay constant attention to them. Almost every experienced turkey hunter has an anecdote about an angry jay, a snorting deer, or a startled rabbit that spooked a turkey and ruined a near-perfect setup. To the truly alert turkey hunter, though, other animals contribute to more successes than failures.

As an example, a few seasons ago in south-central Ohio, a flock of angry crows led me straight to a gobbler. It could have been a deer, an owl, or even a cow that those crows were harassing on the edge of a meadow before sunrise, but I had a strong hunch that it was a turkey, and the hunch proved correct. As the big gobbler strutted along the edge of a clover patch, a crowd of angry crows gathered in the trees along the edge of the field and circled over his head, raising a fuss that could be heard all over the valley. Not ten minutes after I slipped in and set up, the gobbler stepped onto a logging road in front of me in full strut, and I let down the hammer on my muzzleloader to fill my tag.

On a hunt in southeastern Indiana, I stood up to leave the woods, having given up on a gobbler I had played cat and mouse with all morning. As I got up, a pair of Canada geese came flying low over a pasture below me, honking continuously. I stopped to listen and heard what I was sure was the tag end of an answering gobble between honks. I slipped into a good spot near one corner of the pasture and began calling quietly. The bird never gobbled again, but perhaps fifteen minutes later I spotted his white head bobbing through the woods toward me. He stopped forty yards out, and I bowled him over with a load of copper-plated No. 5s.

Experience can train us to see and hear better, and to correctly interpret what we see and hear. The best woodsmen seem to see and hear everything. They catch the subtle sounds of a squirrel's claws on hickory bark, and recognize the sound for what it is. They hear every leaf that rustles and every twig that pops. If stones click in a creek bottom, they hear them and know that something is crossing the creek. They see a whitetail's ear flutter in a thicket eighty yards out and spot a raccoon peeking out of a den in a beech tree. If the quarry is wild boar, they smell a wallow on the breeze. If the breeze shifts, they feel it. Sometimes it's the lack of sound that is a tip-off. If the woods grow suddenly quiet, watch out.

Time Out

One simple step any hunter can take to increase his level of awareness is to leave his watch behind. The turkeys aren't on a clock, and that is one of their chief advantages over hunters. Try your best to forget about time. If a delay keeps you out of the woods until well after first light, don't let it affect your attitude. If you have any sense of frustration related to when you get afield, how much time you have to spend there, or when you have to leave, do your best to shed it. It's not always possible to forget about time, I know. In many states hunters must be aware of legal hunting hours that end at noon or one o'clock.

Hunters have obligations requiring them to be home by a certain time. They hunt with buddies, and they need to coordinate their schedules. To the extent possible, though, try to forget about time. You know that time is elastic--minutes can crawl by like hours, hours can fly by like minutes. Whether you have two hours to hunt or two weeks, do your best to disengage from time for that period. When you succeed, you will be moving to the same rhythms as the animals you hunt. You will not only see more game, you will see more game that is relaxed and unaware of your presence.

One habit I've found helpful when I can't leave my watch at home or in camp is to set the alarm to alert me when it's time to leave. The likelihood that game will hear and react to the tiny beeping of my watch is remote; even if game could hear the sound, the freedom to forget about time and become totally absorbed in the here and now would make it well worthwhile. Ascetics overcome distractions and improve concentration by learning to disengage their minds from pain and discomfort. I have sat motionless as spiders crawled over my face, resisted nearly overwhelming urges to sneeze, cough, or clear my throat, and even let my bladder expand to unhealthful proportions because I heard or saw game approaching. This sort of discipline is shared by most serious hunters. Still, I'm not recommending asceticism for its own sake. In fact, I suggest trying the opposite: whenever possible, achieve relaxation and heightened awareness through physical comfort, which I believe is an underrated aspect of turkey hunting--or any other kind of hunting. It is far easier to forget about time and tune in to your environment if you're comfortable. Comfort means dressing properly for the weather, picking a suitable set-up spot, and taking the time to get set up properly. For many turkey hunters, comfort means a cushion of some sort to keep them off the hard, wet ground, and possibly a vest with padding in the back, to lean against. Find out what it takes to make you comfortable in the woods, and do it.

I know one hunter with chronic back problems who simply cannot sit comfortably against a tree. After years of discomfort, leaving set-ups too quickly, and fidgeting, he began carrying a fold-up seat into the woods. He has to choose his setups a little more carefully and use his pruning shears to provide additional concealment, but his success on turkeys and his enjoyment of turkey hunting has gone up dramatically.

If you are fidgety by nature, breathing exercises can help. After you've situated yourself and gotten comfortable, concentrate on breathing very slowly and deeply for two or three minutes to relax. If you've never tried it, you might be surprised how well this can work. Many hunters cannot enter the woods without fretting that they have arrived later than they wanted to and have missed prime time, or must leave earlier than they would like to. The weather was always better yesterday for some hunters, when they couldn't get out - -unless it's perfect today, in which case they worry that they had better fill their tag quickly because rain is in the forecast for tomorrow. Other hunters cannot shuck the stresses of the workaday world, worrying about project deadlines, conflicts with coworkers, bills, and so forth. Some are so conditioned by the emphasis on productivity that they cannot avoid anxiety while afield when they could be working, mowing the lawn, repairing a leaky faucet, changing the oil in their vehicle, or any of the inexhaustible supply of chores. Still others experience no awareness of stress or anxiety, but cannot stop the internal dialogue that runs endlessly through their heads like a radio that cannot be turned off. And perhaps most unfortunate of all are those individuals for whom everything, including leisure and recreational activity, is a competition. They must fill more tags than other hunters, and their turkeys must have longer beards and spurs. If not (or so they imagine), their reputations as turkey slayers will suffer.

These are common problems that sap our energy, keep us from focusing on the here and now, prevent us from being fully aware of our surroundings, and rob us from totally enjoying the outdoor experience. When you head into the woods, use whatever mental strategies you can that will help you overcome them. I've mentioned deep breathing, and the example of my deer hunting friend who sits with his eyes closed for ten minutes before beginning to hunt.

Another solution might be as simple as giving yourself a gift. For however much time you have available -- a few hours, half a day, a day, or more -- tell yourself that it is your time and no one else's. You are giving it to yourself. Or, you might try simply reminding yourself that you're in the woods, that for a period of time there is nothing you can do about any problems you might be inclined to worry about. Or that you hunt in part for your health -- to get exercise and fresh air, relieve stress, relax -- and that by worrying, you are defeating the very purpose for being there.

When you've forgotten about time, gotten comfortable, and relaxed, and emptied your head of all the workaday stresses and worries that burden most of us much of the time, you'll be ready to hunt. You will see and hear more. You will learn faster. You will hunt with more confidence. You'll be fully engaged in what you're doing, focused solely on the here and now, alert to everything going on around you. Call it heightened awareness, call it an alpha state, attribute it to primal hunting instincts or even mystical powers if you like, but when you get there you will find yourself making intuitive decisions that will usually put you in range of your quarry. At times, you'll swear you can sense the approach of game. You'll feel less like an intruder in the natural world, more like a part of it. It's such a fantastic feeling, and the fact that you're achieving more hunting success will be incidental.

155

Deep frying whole turkeys, a traditional method in the South, keeps turkeys juicy and makes for a golden brown, appetizing presentation. It's also quick and easy.

"I went to the woods because I wished to live deliberately, to front only the essential facts of life, and see if I could not learn what it had to teach, and not, when I came to die, discover that I had not lived."

--Henry David Thoreau, Walden, 1854

Chapter 18

THE SECOND BEST PART OF TURKEY HUNTING

That would be eating the turkey, of course. Wild turkey is superior to any farm-raised turkey, with a flavor that is fuller and at the same time more subtle and complex. Two caveats apply to the preparation of wild turkey, regardless of the cooking method. First, as with any game, proper preparation begins in the field. That means cooling the bird down as quickly as possible. Hanging the turkey by one leg in a shady area for fifteen or twenty minutes will cool it considerably. If it will be more than two hours or so before the bird can be fully cleaned, eviscerating it in the field is a good idea. Pluck some feathers around the vent, carefully make a cut between the vent and the sternum, then slice down toward the vent and cut a hole around it, removing the intestines and taking care not to cut them or tear them open.

Second, wild turkeys are not self-basting. If they get dry, they become tough and flavorless. Preventing this does not require extraordinary measures, but wild turkeys require a little more attention than do their domestic counterparts, which stay moist because they are fat or because they have had oils or fats injected into them.

For reasons that mystify me, it is common to smoke, barbecue, marinade, or heavily spice wild turkey; my own belief is that the wild turkey's delicate flavor may be judiciously enhanced or complemented, but it is doubtful it can be improved upon. With that in mind, here are some recipes that I believe best bring out the naturally delicious flavor of wild turkeys.

The first two recipes will impress any dinner guests, and they're easy to make. They involve classic crepes, so we'll start with a basic recipe for those. Keep in mind that after it is made, crepe batter can be stored in the refrigerator for at least two days, and can be thinned as needed with milk. Finished crepes can be refrigerated or frozen. It is not necessary to put waxed paper or similar materials between crepes, but they are easier to separate if they are offset, and not stacked precisely atop one another.

Classic Crepes

Ingredients

2 eggs
2 tablespoons melted butter
1-1/3 cups milk
1 cup flour
dash of salt

Place all the ingredients in a blender in the order listed, and blend on high for about 25 seconds. Scrape batter down the sides of the blender and blend for a few more seconds. Prepare a crepe pan (a small, 6- or 7-inch skillet will work) by seasoning or using no-stick spray shortening. Put 1/2 teaspoon of butter in the pan for the first crepe only. The crepe batter should not be too thin, but should run freely enough to cover the bottom of the pan when about 3 tablespoons of batter are poured in and the pan is tilted. (If you pour in too much, the excess can be poured back out. If the entire crepe pours out of the pan, the temperature is not yet high enough.) The temperature is right when a crepe will cook on one side in one minute or so. Color should be tan or pale brown, not dark.

When it begins to get crisp around the edges, loosen it with a spatula, pick up an edge carefully with your fingers, and flip it. Don't worry if there is a flap; it won't show when the crepe is rolled. If it tears when you lift it, it's not ready to turn.

If the pan sticks, wipe it with a paper towel and put butter or more non-stick spray shortening on it. If this is your first time making crepes, you might need to experiment a little to get the temperature and consistency of the batter just right, but soon you'll be turning them out like a pro. This recipe should make about a dozen 6-inch crepes.

Wild Turkey and Broccoli Crepes

You won't find this recipe anywhere else. I won't claim to have invented it. Like most recipes, I suppose, it evolved over time; in this case an adaptation of an earlier recipe for a more common fowl, with a slight change here, an addition there. Serve it with a crisp white wine.

Ingredients

1-1/2 cups grated sharp cheddar cheese
8 crepes   Salt and pepper
3 tablespoons butter   2 cups cooked, cubed turkey
3 tablespoons flour   8 tablespoons sour cream
1-1/2 cups milk   8 pieces cooked broccoli
2 tablespoons Worcestershire   Parmesan cheese

Melt butter in saucepan over medium heat, add flour and stir, cooking about 2 minutes. Add milk slowly and stir until thick, then add Worcestershire, cheese, salt and pepper lightly. Add turkey cubes. Mix thoroughly.

Spread each crepe with a tablespoon of sour cream, and place a spear of broccoli on sour cream, cover with turkey and sauce, roll up crepe, and place in a buttered or seasoned ovenproof serving dish. Sprinkle Parmesan cheese over the crepes, and bake in oven 375° F for 10 to 15 minutes. Serves 4.

Note: *If the pan sticks, wipe it with a paper towel and put butter or more non-stick spray shortening on it.*

Turkey Mushroom Water Chestnut Crepes

This is NOT how the pilgrims served turkey - but what did they know? You'll need a wine sauce for this recipe, but it's quick and easy:

Wine Sauce Ingredients

1/4 cup butter
1/4 cup flour
1/4 cup dry sherry or dry vermouth
2 cups milk
1 tablespoon Worcestershire sauce
Salt and white pepper

Melt the butter over medium heat and add flour, stirring 2 minutes. Slowly stir in sherry, milk, Worcestershire, salt and pepper, until sauce thickens. Keep warm.

<u>Filling Ingredients</u>

8 crepes, above	1/4 cup chopped pimientos
Wine sauce	4 water chestnuts, diced
1/4 cup butter	2 cups diced cooked turkey
2 cups sliced button mushrooms	Paprika
6 green onions/scallions, slice thinly	

Melt butter in skillet, add mushrooms, and sauté for 4 minutes. Add onions and cook until translucent-about 3 minutes. Add pimientos, water chestnuts, and turkey. Add enough wine sauce to moisten, then fill each crepe with turkey mixture. Roll and put in buttered oven-proof serving dish, top with rest of wine sauce, sprinkle with paprika. Bake for 10 minutes at 375° F. If desired, turn on broiler after baking to brown top lightly. Serves 4.

Wine-Braised Wild Turkey

Coq Au Vin is a classic French dish. This recipe substitutes wild turkey for chicken. Don't be intimidated by the long list of ingredients - this dish is as simple as adding ingredients to the pot and cooking. First, fillet turkey breasts and cut into serving-size cutlets.

Melt 3 tablespoons of butter, then add and brown:
1/4 lb. minced salt pork
1/2 cup pearl onions
3 minced shallots
1 carrot, sliced
1 peeled garlic clove

Add turkey and brown, then stir in:

2 tablespoons flour
2 tablespoons parsley, minced
1/2 bay leaf
1 tablespoons marjoram
1/2 teaspoon thyme
Dash salt
1/8 teaspoon pepper

Add and stir in:

1-1/2 cups dry red wine

Cook over low heat, covered, for about 1 hour, then add:

1/3 to 1/2 lb. sliced mushrooms

Cook mushrooms for 5 minutes or so, skim off excess fat from salt pork, then serve turkey topped with sauce and other ingredients.

Simply Stuffed Wild Turkey

Everyone has a favorite turkey stuffing, but sometimes the simplest recipe is the best.

Ingredients

1 dressed wild turkey	3 sliced apples
Lemon juice	1/2 cup chopped celery
1/3 cup butter	1/2 cup vegetable oil
3 tablespoons flour	Salt and pepper

Clean turkey thoroughly with cold water, rub salt and pepper on inside of bird. Melt butter and stir in flour and pepper to make a paste. Spread paste over turkey. Stuff turkey with apples and celery, and tie.

Baste frequently with vegetable oil and lemon juice mixture. Roast about 2 hours, depending on size of the bird.

Wild Rice Turkey Soup

Here's one excellent way to use leftover turkey, or the parts that are often discarded.

Ingredients

Turkey legs, neck, giblets, or carcass with meat	
4 cups cooked wild rice	1/4 onion, chopped
9 cups water	2 carrots, chopped
Pinch of parsley	Bay leaf
1/2 teaspoon thyme	Salt and pepper

Cut carcass apart, and place in a pot with water. Bring to boil. Add rest of ingredients except rice. Simmer two hours.

Remove carcass from water, strip meat, and put back into soup. Skim fat from surface. Add rice. Simmer another 20 minutes. Leftovers freeze well.

Cream-Roasted Turkey

Season it lightly and serve it by candlelight with a full-bodied Chardonnay if you wish, but it's hard to beat with biscuits and beer in a cabin after a cool, rainy spring day of turkey hunting.

Ingredients

Dressed turkey	Butter
Flour	Cream
Salt and pepper	

Cut turkey into serving sizes, rinse and pat dry. Dredge in flour, salt, and pepper. Fry in butter until lightly browned. Put in roasting pan, add just enough cream to cover pieces of turkey. Bake at 350° F, about 20 minutes for each pound of turkey.

Turkey Stuffed With Wild Rice

Ingredients

Dressed turkey	1 teaspoon salt
Lemon juice	2 cups mushrooms
3 cups water	1/4 cup chopped celery
1-1/2 cups wild rice	1/4 cup butter
1/2 cup onion, chopped	1 tablespoon poultry seasoning
1 tablespoon bacon fat	1/2 cup stewed tomatoes

Rinse and dry turkey, then rub inside with lemon juice. Rinse rice under cold water, drain, put in pot. Bring 3 cups water to a boil, and pour over rice, then add salt and simmer for one hour, adding more water if necessary. Drain rice.

Over low heat in frying pan, melt butter and bacon fat. Sauté mushrooms, onions, celery. In a mixing bowl, pour in tomatoes and seasonings. Add rice and mushroom mixture. Stuff the turkey, then put in roasting pan. Pour 2 cups of water over turkey, cover bird loosely with aluminum foil, and bake at 350° F until tender.

Turkey season coincides with mushroom season in many areas, and it only makes sense to take advantage of that happy coincidence by collecting fresh morels when turkey hunting. (Morels are the easiest to identify and safest to pick of all the mushrooms, but you'll want to be confident about picking morels before trying these recipes.) The simplest recipe: throw 10 morels, fresh or dried, along with a cup of water, into the pan for the last hour when you bake a turkey for great gravy. That advice comes from mushroom expert Larry Lonik. The next two recipes are adapted from Lonik's book <u>Basically Morels</u>. See www.morelheaven.com for additional morel recipes.

Pan Turkey and Morels

<u>Ingredients</u>

3 pounds turkey pieces
Seasoned flour
4 tablespoons butter
2 tablespoons oil
1/3 cup dry white wine
1-1/2 pounds morels cleaned, sliced

4 cups heavy cream
1 large egg yolk
Salt
Freshly ground black pepper
Lemon juice (optional)

Dredge the turkey in seasoned flour and brown lightly in butter and oil. A sauté pan of at least 14" would be preferable. Add wine and cook until wine is almost evaporated, turning the turkey occasionally. Add morels and cream and cook, uncovered, until turkey is done. Remove, with as many morels as possible, to a hot serving dish. Boil down the sauce by half, and thicken by beating the egg yolk with a little of the sauce, then cook it all together, just below boiling, for about 5 minutes. Season to taste with salt and pepper. Lemon juice may be added. Pour over turkey and serve. Rice goes well with this dish.

Roast Turkey and Morels

<u>Ingredients</u>

1 roasted turkey
1-1/2 cups morels, sliced lengthwise
2 tablespoons turkey drippings
2 tablespoons butter

Salt
2 tablespoons flour
1 teaspoon lemon juice
1 teaspoon chopped fresh parsley
1 1/2 cups heavy cream

Carve turkey into servings, keep warm. In a skillet, sauté morels in drippings and butter over low heat for 5 minutes. Sprinkle with salt and push to side of pan. Stir in flour until smooth, then mix together with morels and continue to cook another 2 minutes. Stir in cream until it thickens. Add lemon juice and parsley. Pour over turkey and serve immediately.

Southern-Style Deep-Fried Turkey

Deep frying turkeys, a tradition in the South, is catching on elsewhere. Deep fryers are made specifically for this, but however you do it, keep safety in mind when working with a large container of hot oil. Here's one simple but delicious technique.

<u>Ingredients</u>

Turkey
Seasonings (salt and pepper)

Determine the right amount of oil to use by putting the turkey into the pot, and covering it with water, leaving a minimum of 4 inches below the rim. (If covering the bird leaves less than 4 inches to the rim, the pot is not big enough.) Take the bird out and mark the level of the water with the bird out of the pot. Then pour out the water and dry the pot, add oil (peanut oil is a favorite) up to the mark, and heat it to 350° F.

Make sure turkey is completely dry. Season the turkey inside and out while the oil is heating. Wire the drumsticks together with good, sturdy wire. You must be confident the wire will support the weight of the turkey and not slip off.

When the oil is hot enough, use a long hook to carefully lower the turkey into it. Cook 3 minutes per pound, then use the hook to lift the turkey, letting it drain over the pot. Place it on paper towels to catch oil.

As a variation on the above, turkeys needn't be fried whole. Slice turkey breast into finger-size strips, dredge in seasoned flour, and fry in hot oil in a skillet.

Here's a delicious way to use those inevitable little scraps of turkey that have to be picked off the bones after you slice the bird.

Fruited Turkey Salad

<u>Ingredients</u>

1-1/2 cups cut-up cooked turkey
1 cup seedless green grapes
1 8-oz. can water chestnuts, drained & chopped
1 11-oz. can mandarin orange segments, drained

1/2 cup mayonnaise
1/2 teaspoon salt
1/4 teaspoon curry powder

Combine turkey, grapes, water chestnuts, orange segments. Mix remaining ingredients and toss with turkey mixture. Serves 4.

Turkey-Vegetable Fondue

Ever notice how guests congregate in the kitchen while you cook? With a fondue, you cut to the chase and everyone cooks his or her own. It's a fun, easy, and sociable way to serve a medium-size group.

<u>Ingredients</u>

2 lbs. turkey breasts in bite-size pieces   4 -5 cups cooked rice
1 lb. broccoli flowerettes   8 cups chicken broth
8 oz. mushrooms, sliced
Lemon-soy sauce (1/2 cup soy sauce, 1 bunch green onions, cut in 1/2-inch pieces, 1/2 cup lemon juice, 1/4 cup dry white wine)

Put turkey, broccoli, onions, and mushrooms on serving tray. Put hot rice in 8 small bowls.

Heat broth in fondue pot. (An electric skillet will work. I find one pot or skillet ideal for 2-4 people, and prefer to separate into two pots for 6 or 8.) Guests spear turkey or other foods with fondue forks or chopsticks, and hold food in hot broth for 2 or 3 minutes until done, then dip in lemon-soy sauce. After main course, ladle broth over any rice remaining in bowls and eat as soup. Serves 8.